S0-DOO-733

How You Can Manage Your MONEY

How You Can Manage Your MONEY

A Christian's Guide
to Personal and
Family Financial
Decision Making

John
Warren
Johnson

AUGSBURG Publishing House • Minneapolis

HOW YOU CAN MANAGE YOUR MONEY

Copyright © 1981 Augsburg Publishing House

Library of Congress Catalog Card No. 80-67798

International Standard Book No. 0-8066-1860-4

All rights reserved. No part of this book may be used or re-produced in any manner whatsoever without written permis-sion except in the case of brief quotations embodied in critical articles and reviews. For information address Augsburg Publish-ing House, 426 South Fifth Street, Minneapolis, Minnesota 55415.

Scripture quotations unless otherwise noted are from the Good News Bible, Today's English Version: Copyright © American Bible Society 1966, 1971, 1976 and are used by permission.

Scripture quotations marked RSV are from the Revised Standard Version of the Bible, copyright 1946, 1952, and 1971 by the Division of Christian Education and the National Council of Churches.

Manufactured in the United States of America

This book has been written to glorify God and is dedicated to my mother and father, Eileen and Walter E. Johnson, for first teaching me the principles of Christian financial management; to my wife, Marion, who is an expert practitioner of those principles; and to my son, Daniel, and his wife, Terri, who are building the financial part of their marriage on them.

Contents

Why Financial Management Is Important

A pastor called me one day to ask if I would meet with two of his church members on the verge of divorce because of serious personal financial problems. I told him I'd be happy to do so, thinking it would be relatively easy to straighten out their finances and so help save their marriage.

But although I've been teaching classes on personal financial management for years, I discovered it was much easier to tell people what they should do than to get them to do it. My meeting with this couple in my office left me convinced that their financial mess was the result of other things, and not the cause of their marital problems. In spite of my attempts to help them I couldn't even get them to cooperate long enough to make an accurate list of everything they owed. It wasn't long before they started divorce proceedings.

I realized then that financial problems are really intermingled with the whole way in which people live. The problems start with young people growing up with almost no training in money management. They go to school for 12 to 16 years, take many courses that teach them how to earn money, but in most cases none on how to spend it. They learn that as they go along—by the trial and error

9

method. The fact that so many Americans are in serious personal financial trouble is a good indication that they make many errors during the trial process.

As my pastor friends sent more financially troubled people to me, I began to recognize that those with a deep Christian commitment were much more likely to work tenaciously together to solve their financial problems. This led me more deeply into the Bible to pull out all of the personal financial management advice given there. I discovered that the Bible is rich in sound, practical financial guidance, and I realized that anyone who would follow those teachings would not have financial problems.

So I started applying scriptural teaching in the advice I was giving in counseling. Some amazing things began to happen. People who thought my suggestions were "nice ideas" concluded that if the Bible said these things, then they had to be more than nice ideas; they were authentic guidelines.

I also discovered that what many people accept as ordinary common sense, such as buying second-hand furniture, shopping at garage sales, or knowing where you can double the interest on your savings, are brand new ideas to many.

Although the Bible clearly spells out many financial principles, it does not do so in 20th-century language. When it was written, there were no such things as "Investor's Certificates" or five classes of home-owners' insurance. But basic biblical principles fit all of these proliferating new developments. Once we understand and use these principles, it is relatively easy to apply them to our situations.

As with every other aspect of our lives, what the Bible teaches us about finances really works. These principles have worked far beyond anything I could have anticipated in my own life, in the lives of my family members, and in the lives of many other Christians.

Yet, millions of people are suffering extreme and unnecessary personal financial hardships. I have written this book to help people understand what the Bible says about personal financial management, and to encourage them to apply its principles to all of their everyday personal financial decisions. If it encourages them to follow these biblical teachings, it will help lift the heavy burden of financial worry from many people. And if that happens, it will be to God's glory.

THE WAY IS EASY

It's easy to spend ourselves into real financial trouble. The Bible recognizes this in many ways.

Jesus said, "Enter by the narrow gate; for the gate is wide and the way is easy, that leads to destruction, and those who enter by it are many. For the gate is narrow and the way is hard, that leads to life, and those who find it are few" (Matt. 7:13-14 RSV). Although this passage refers to the new life in Christ, it is appropriate to apply it to the way in which people handle their own finances. The gate to spending more than we earn is wide open, and with small down payments, easy credit, small monthly installments, deferred payment plans, checking plus, and all the rest, "the way is easy that leads to [financial] destruction."

Christians know this, yet many have established a spending and consumption pattern in which they spend every cent every payday and have committed more and more future paychecks long before they arrive. The absolute danger point for committing future paychecks for non-real-estate installment debt payments alone is 20% of your take-home pay. And that's really stretching things to the limit. But millions of Americans have committed themselves to paying much more than 20%, with little regard for whether they will even have a job when those payments come due next month, next year, or even two and three years from now.

The Bible again gives sound advice, which many people have recognized only after they've learned it the hard way. Jesus told of the prodigal son's problem: "He spent everything he had. Then a severe famine spread over that country, and he was left without a thing" (Luke 15:14).

We could paraphrase that to read, "He spent everything he had, and then came . . . job loss, cutback in overtime, illness, car breakdown, unexpected rent increases, and a dozen other problems for which no provision had been made."

People see great material wealth all around them. The family living on one side of the street has two nice cars; the family on the other, a big new recreational vehicle; the family next to them, a beautiful new boat; and the family across the street, a new lake cottage. With everyone else seemingly able to buy so much, it's only normal that people ask themselves, "Why not me, too?"

What they don't know is that the neighbor with the two new cars probably has two 42-month loans to pay off, and might already be lying awake nights trying to figure out how to make the next payment. The people with the recreational vehicle might have just discovered that they'll have time and money to drive it only about three weeks each year and will have to pay to store it the other 49. And about this time, they may be thinking of ways in which they can rent it out to get enough money to make monthly payments, plus pay for repairs, license fees, and insurance. The couple with the new boat could have unwittingly committed themselves to eating peanut butter sandwiches and macaroni casseroles for the next three years to pay for it. Things are never so rosy as they look when they are in the hands of people who have put material wealth first in their lives.

Christians should put God first in their lives. Once they have managed to make that commitment, all of these other "things" become *relatively* unimportant. When they are relatively unimportant, they will not dominate a Christian's life. As Paul said, "I have learned to be satisfied with what I have" (Phil. 4:11). Or, as another Scripture says, "Be satisfied with what you have" (Heb. 13:5).

Phil. 4:11
Heb. 13:5

Financial problems are also one of the major contributors to family breakups and family cruelty. One research project concluded that 40% of desertion cases were caused by financial tensions between husband and wife, while 45% of the cruelty cases were caused by tension brought on by financial problems.

WARNING SIGNALS

If you are like many Americans, you may think you are not in a real financial hole, but at the same time aren't sure whether you can continue the balancing and juggling act. Here are some warning signals that will tell you whether or not you are in trouble and need help:

1. You find it more and more difficult each month to make ends meet.

2. You rely heavily on overtime pay and income from a second job.

3. You pay only the minimum due on your charge-account bills, and sometimes juggle payments, stalling one creditor to pay another.

4. You have to struggle to save even small amounts and don't have enough set aside to get you through such upsets as a pay cut or the need to replace even a minor appliance.

5. You use credit to pay for everyday expenses you once covered with cash.

6. You use the cash-advance feature of your bank card or take out another kind of loan to pay bills.

7. You get past-due notices with some bills.

8. You find yourself using the "checking plus" feature of your checking account more and more frequently. If you find yourself in one or more of these situations, you should know that it's time to slow down before it's too late.

This book suggests some ways in which you can get your finances back under control if they are slipping beyond your grasp. At the same time, it provides guidelines for those who have not reached the point of real trouble. Perhaps you are just starting out as newlyweds and are looking for guidance on financial matters, such as whether or not you should buy a home or a new car, whether you should put your money into a savings account or some other form of investment, where you should go to buy your furniture, and how much you should spend on housing.

The Bible will be the principal authority in this book. It contains guidance for every financial question. Among the many things the Bible teaches us about spending are these:

1. Our motives in spending are important to God. "Do not love the world or anything that belongs to the world. If you love the world, you do not love the Father. Everything that belongs to the world—what the sinful self desires, what people see and want, and everything in this world that people are so proud of—none of this comes from the Father; it all comes from the world" (1 John 2:15-16).

2. Spending apart from a commitment to God will not satisfy. "Instead, be concerned above everything else

had to go out and find an apartment of their own. The only one they could afford was unfurnished, except for a refrigerator and range, but at least they thought they could handle the rent on top of the car payments and still have enough left for food and gasoline.

After they'd been in their apartment a few days, with only their sleeping bags, their old set of dishes and bath towels, they decided "this was no way to live." Driving by a credit furniture store, they saw they could buy "three full rooms" of furniture for only $875, with no money down. Their eyes lit up, they signed another contract with only 12 "easy payments" of $89 each, and the furniture arrived. How happy they were to have a bed to sleep in, a couch to sit on, and a television set to watch, even if it was only a 17-incher.

Ten months after they were married, their first baby arrived. In the meantime, both of them had received small increases in their wages and had been late in their payments for the rent, Olds, and furniture only three times each. But they were managing to stay just close enough in their payments that nothing had been repossessed and they had not been evicted.

John had some insurance through his employer, but discovered that it did not cover all hospital and doctor expenses and ended up with a bill of $285. The hospital wouldn't let Mary and the baby out until he paid the bill, but finally agreed to release them after he signed a promissory note to pay it off in three equal monthly installments.

John and Mary didn't know how they were going to make those monthly payments on top of the car, furniture, food, gas, and rent, but they were so happy with the new baby they didn't really give it much thought.

During the following nine months John and Mary learned how to tell the car finance company that "the check was just mailed yesterday." They also learned how to mail a check without signing it, knowing it would have to be returned to them for signature and they could gain a little more time.

They learned that the finance company, to whom the contract on the furniture had been sold, was willing to write a new loan on the furniture. However, they did something called "recomputing the precompute." John wasn't sure what it meant, but he did know that the old loan had only three months to go and the new one now stretched out to another full 12-month period.

He decided it was time to cut his high cost of living and the car was the place to start. He was paying a dollar a day to park his big car, but had discovered it was possible to park behind his place of employment free of charge, if he had a motorcycle. Through a coincidence he saw a sale on demonstrator motorcycles with no down payment, and the balance due in 18 "easy payments." John jumped at the chance.

Sixty days later, their second baby arrived.

Unfortunately, John had not been able to complete payment to the first hospital and doctor, so he and Mary had to use a second hospital and a second gynecologist. When the day came to bring their new son home, they were held up in the hospital credit office as they went through the now familiar procedure of signing a promissory note for the balance above the amount covered by the insurance. They had not yet learned one of the Bible's financial warnings, "Sensible people will see trouble coming and avoid it, but an unthinking person will walk right into it and regret it later" (Prov. 22:3).

When John and Mary got home that night, they finally sat down and added up what they owed and how much they were supposed to be paying each month. They still had payments on the Olds, the motorcycle, the hospital for the first baby, the finance company on the furniture, and now the new installments due the hospital for the second baby. They were stunned when they discovered the total monthly payments they had promised to make were $785. Mary was now unemployed and John's total monthly take-home pay was only $662.85. It wouldn't even cover the payments, much less their living expenses.

For more than a week they lay awake late into the night talking about their problem and soon started to blame it on each other. If only the babies hadn't come along, Mary would still be working. But then, if only John hadn't bought that big car, and if only Mary hadn't wanted shiny new furniture, and if only John hadn't bought that motorcycle, and on it went.

After two almost sleepless weeks, they came to my office.

Does the story sound extreme? To many it would be, but others can identify with it immediately. Thousands of couples find themselves in the same position. We'll look at this kind of situation more closely in Chapter 8.

Many other young people are on the verge of making similar initial errors. One such couple, who are both relatively well established financially, is planning to be married soon. Bill is 27 years old, and he has been out of college and employed for four years. Jane is 23, graduated from college a year ago, and has a good job.

They are sensible, intelligent, down-to-earth people who got off to a good start after finishing school. But they've already made three significant money-management errors that could cause them financial problems for years to come.

After Bill graduated, he and a friend decided to buy a single-family home and live in it together. In this way, they would both build up equity and take advantage of the steadily increasing price of houses. They pooled their savings, made a minimum down payment, and bought a nice home. It was a wise decision.

However, in the transaction Bill made his first mistake. The two men had decided that Bill's friend would be the sole owner of the house if either of them decided he wanted out of the partnership. If Bill was the first to leave, his half interest in the house would be bought by his friend, and if the friend wanted out, they would sell to a third party. The purchase agreement said only that they would have two independent appraisals made at the time of the buy-out, and would average them to fix the sale price. This is not so bad, but it would have been better if the agreement called for a third appraisal in the event the first two were more than 5% apart.

But the real loophole in the purchase agreement was that Bill would receive only "a substantial part of his equity" at the time of the buy-out. "Substantial part" was not defined and could be interpreted as low as 10% or 15%. Bill's equity represented about 90% of his total assets, and it was from that equity that he would have money to buy a house for his bride and himself, if they were going to have one of their own.

The second and third errors, both common, were to purchase two new cars. Neither Bill nor Jane could buy for cash, so each bought on the installment plan. Both signed 42-month contracts and committed a significant part of their take-home pay for the next three and one-half years.

Here was an intelligent, well-educated, and competent young couple, who could have entered marriage with two used cars (preferably one) and Bill's equity in the house (approximately $10,000). Yet they were about to be married with only $2000 in cash as the "substantial payment" from the house, and the two three-and-a-half-year installment contracts with combined monthly payments of $327.

Bill's settlement with his partner netted him $2000 cash plus monthly payments from the second mortgage which the buyer had given them at 8%. So most of his personal funds were tied up in that mortgage. Bill and Jane had dug themselves into a financial hole by virtue of his overlooking a potential problem and their wanting to start their marriage with two new cars.

Both have above-average earning power and, after two or three years in an apartment, if they manage carefully, they can have the cars paid for and have enough saved to make a down payment on a house. Another alternative is to take the second mortgage to a bank and use it as security for a loan, and then use the loan to make the down payment on a home. This might be their best route, but they'd have to pay the bank much more than 8% interest for the loan. We'll suggest some other alternatives for Bill and Jane in Chapter 3.

WORKING SINGLES

When Kathy Smith and her husband divorced, she was paid $3000, a somewhat unusual lump-sum settlement. They gave up their expensive apartment because neither had the advantage of two salaries to draw on. Kathy went off by herself and rented a less expensive apartment. Her income was adequate to pay all of her living expenses and, fortunately, both she and her husband had paid-up cars before the divorce.

Kathy's main financial problem was what to do with the $3000. She knew that if she spent it, the only reserve she had for emergencies would be gone. She also knew that if she put it into a 5½% savings passbook account, with inflation running double that rate, her $3000 would drop in purchasing power by $150 per year.

She had learned that banks and savings and loans were selling savings certificates which were tied to the interest rate paid by the federal government. That interest rate was around 10% at the time, which sounded good to her. But then Kathy was told she would need at least $10,000 to buy the minimum-size certificate under this program. She had heard that some people were combining their savings to build the amount up to the $10,000 so they could get the 10% interest. Then they shared the interest at the end of each 180-day maturity period and stayed even with inflation.

Kathy also learned that she could buy "government paper" through her banker or a stockbroker. She'd never bought any stock before, so she didn't have a broker. Her banker told her she could invest money in government paper in quantities as low as $1000, and for periods of time as short as a few days. The yield from the interest would be around 10%. This sounded as good as joining a $10,000 Investors Certificate Club, because she could be on her own. And the minimum required for these investments was only $1000.

Then Kathy thought of the stock market. She was vaguely aware that most stock prices hadn't moved very much for several years. But she had read that some corporations were making all-time record profits and, consequently, paying all-time record dividends. She decided to look into it.

She discovered she could buy well-known stocks like American Telephone & Telegraph Co. (A.T.&T.), Cincinnati Bell Telephone, utilities which supply gas and electricity, and many others that would pay her a dividend four times per year, with a return to her of between 9% and 11% at the current dividend rate and current market price for the stock. She knew there was always the risk of the prices or dividends going down, but after checking with a broker, she discovered the stocks had been stable for a long time and, in the opinion of many people, stock should be selling a good deal higher. So, if those "experts" were correct, she also might just see her $3000 turn into $3500, or maybe $4000, if the stocks would go up 15% or 20% in price.

Then, friends told her about money-market funds, stock-investment funds, municipal bonds, municipal-bond investment funds, second mortgages, contracts for deed, and a dozen other places to invest her $3000. The more she listened, the more confused she became, until she finally decided to leave the money in something she understood—a 5½% passbook savings account.

Her decision would cost her the difference between 5½% and the inflation rate for the year. If the inflation rate was 10½%, she would lose 5% on her $3000 per year in cash income and in terms of what that $3000 would eventually buy. So her money was shrinking at a real $150 in the first year, down to $2850. The second year it would drop $142.50, shrinking her $3000 down to $2707.50. And with her money in a passbook account, it wouldn't be too many years before her $3000 would provide little in the way of a financial reserve. But other alternatives were open to Kathy, and they aren't hard to take or risky. Chapter 10 suggests a step-by-step plan that Kathy could follow.

Terry Bates is another single working person. Her husband had died recently, leaving her little but their furniture in their rented home, and a $9000, two-year, 6½% savings certificate. Terry's income was adequate to pay the rent, and she wisely chose to stay put with her two growing children living at home. The rent was less than would have been needed for a much smaller space in an apartment building. Her income would take care of her living expenses, although there was little left for luxuries. But, by buying only what was really necessary, taking advantage of garage sales and used-clothing sales, and shopping carefully at the grocery stores, she was able to make ends meet.

Her reserve was the $9000 savings certificate. She knew that the value of it was dropping by 4% per year, at the current $10^1/2$% rate of inflation, and that little by little the $9000 was shrinking.

She was only $1000 short of the $10,000 required for the 10%, 120-day investor certificates and, if she could just come up with the additional $1000, she could take advantage of a savings possibility that would almost keep her even with inflation. She wasn't aware that a stock brokerage house would take any amount over $1000 and invest it in a money-market fund. But she had heard of second mortgages and contracts for deed, and decided to learn more. (See Chapter 11.)

Alice Olson is the divorced mother of three children. Her husband has disappeared and, even though the court had ordered him to make child-support payments, none are coming. Alice doesn't even know where to look for her ex-husband, so she's on her own, and she has some real problems.

She could go on welfare and get money from the "aid to families of dependent children" program, but she doesn't want that. However, because her earning power is limited and there will be an extra expense for day care for the one preschool child, she knows she'll need some outside help.

Her biggest problem is housing. No one will rent an apartment to a mother with three children because of the harder wear on the building. Other tenants might object to the noise, and the landlord does not want to lose them.

But even if a landlord would take her with her children, the rent would be more than she could afford.

But there are some answers for Alice, and we'll look at them in more detail in Chapter 2.

Bill James has created quite a different problem for himself. He likes to "live life to the hilt." This world is here to enjoy," he said. "I'll worry about tomorrow when it comes." So he borrowed money for elaborate vacations, including a three-week stint in Hawaii and another in Europe. He ran up charges to the allowable limits on all his credit cards and bought everything that met his fancy —mostly on credit. Before he knew it, he was deeply in debt.

Here's what happens when you start to go into debt. If you add $1000 a year to your debts for a total of 15 years, and you compound the interest on that debt at only 10% (which is really too low because credit card charges are 18% in most states, and even bank loans today are well over 10%), at the end of 15 years you will owe $34,941. To repay that debt in the same length of time (15 years), you will have to pay back $4000 per year. That's a tremendous amount. But it's that high because you'll continue to pay interest on the balance you owe even while you are trying to reduce it.

Single people face problems that married people don't face and vice versa. Some tax laws discriminate against singles; usually they have only their single salary as a source of income, while married couples frequently have two. Singles face the additional emotional pressure to overcome the loneliness of sitting home alone most nights. But there are ways to lessen their financial problems and to temper the emotional problems that frequently bring on the financial problems.

Bill really needed some help, but mostly he needed

some self-control. In Chapter 9 we'll suggest some solutions.

MATURING COUPLES

Maturing couples subconsciously discover that people never treat you as well as when you're spending money. The delighted waiter who receives the big tip, the head of the fund-raising drive, the golfers who enjoy seeing you pick up the tab on the 19th hole, and the clerk who has just sold you a pair of new shoes—all seem to treat you better.

In a day when instant and immediate results are important, spending works wonders. It brings "instant importance."

To assist this psychological pressure for instant importance, our whole life-style is based on an abundance of things, and enormous pressures are exerted to keep our desire for things foremost in our minds. On an average evening, television watchers are subjected to more than 100 commercials that put pressure on them to buy and spend.

Those who write the commercials know that women are vulnerable to appeals to vanity. Consequently, soap is sold on the basis that you will have nice, white, soft hands rather than because it will do a better job of washing the dishes.

The commercial writers also know that men are susceptible to appeals to their egos. As a result, many men's products are sold by former professional athletes or actors. Although most men never had those glory days, they can become a part of them by buying the pro-athlete's brand. Or, perhaps, a product is sold with a picture of a yacht, decorated with lovely ladies, cruising in the South Pacific. The man in charge is handsome, muscular, deeply tanned, and the kind of a "he-man" many men wish to be. And a few million men troop to the store.

New cars are seldom sold, even today, on the basis of economy. More common are slogans such as, "You'll look great behind the wheel of a . . . ," and there are the ever-present beautiful young ladies sitting, standing, or lounging on or around the vehicle to reinforce that male ego.

This combination of appeals frequently results in maturing couples spending more money than they have coming in, regardless of the income level. One researcher concluded that families earning twice the national average have greater problems paying their bills than families of average income. Our appetites for things are always bigger than our paychecks.

My own experience in dealing with mature couples or singles earning $30,000 or more shows that many are in real financial trouble. One of these couples, Jim and Sally Young, was deeply in debt when I first met them. They owed money all over town. But unlike many of the younger couples, their bills were larger and were for unusual things.

One was a huge bill at the athletic club, and another was a large one at their golf and country club. They'd done some lavish entertaining for a number of golfing guests, at an average of $40 per person, including green fees, electric carts, lunch before, dinner afterward, and always a couple of gift golf balls. They were behind in payments on their two new cars, one of which was a Cadillac, and owed money at some of the finest clothing stores in town. The number of their past-due accounts was the same as most other financially troubled couples; it was just that the totals were so much larger.

It was easy to see there was a great deal of friction between them. During our interview Sally said, "Jim just has to be the big shot wherever he goes. If he'd let someone else pick up the tab once in a while, we'd be a lot better off."

Jim shot back, "Sally treats a checkbook like a best-selling novel. She just can't put it down until she finishes it."

Back and forth they went. Jim bought the new Cadillac "because I have to put up a good front in my real-estate sales work." Sally went out and bought six beautiful new dresses, all on credit, "because I have to look nice when we entertain guests at the club."

It was obvious the financial problem in this family wasn't really the cause of the trouble; it was just a significant by-product. The real causes were psychological. On top of everything, their marriage was coming apart. They had stopped communicating with each other long ago.

As the gray hairs appeared, Jim felt he was losing his manhood, and compensated by playing the role of the big earner and big spender. Sally's buying was largely for revenge, although she admitted it was a struggle to squeeze into her new dresses, which were the same size she had worn 20 years earlier.

"What is the most important thing in your life?" I asked each of them. Both looked blank. It seemed they had really never thought of it. Was it the new Cadillac? The expensive lunches at the athletic club? The temporary friendships gained from taking guests golfing? The new dresses? Was it any of the "things" they had acquired, or the seemingly endless, meaningless, spending whirlpool into which they had been swept?

As we talked, all of these things were examined and rejected.

Interestingly, for the first time, the two of them seemed to be willing to talk almost rationally to each other about spending. There were some sharp remarks, and the sparks flew occasionally, but the more they talked, the more they started to admit that maybe they had their priorities all wrong. In Chapter 9 we'll see how they turned things around.

Clarence and Elaine have a different problem. They are really disturbed by rising costs all around them and feel they are missing a chance to make some really big money. It has become an obsession with them.

Clarence has a good job and a steady history of employment. His salary is significantly above average. Elaine is the mother of three children, but has accepted a part-time job just to "get out of the house" four hours each day.

In spite of having one good full-time income and a smaller part-time income, Clarence and Elaine aren't able to save anything.

They have one big asset (in addition to their jobs, family, health, and personal property) and that is their house. They have owned it for 11 years and have paid the 7% mortgage down to just under $20,000. But from recent sales of neighboring houses, they know their house is worth at least $75,000. That gives them an equity of $55,000, a sizable sum even in times of inflation.

Their problem is that they are deeply disturbed to see that $55,000 "just lying there" and not earning any income. They want to take it out of the house and make money with it. So we looked at it to get the facts in order.

A whole new mortgage on the house at the time they raised the question would have cost 11% per year. This means their monthly interest payments would have increased from $116 (old mortage of 7% x $20,000) to $550 per month (new mortgage of 11% x $60,000). So their first problem would have been to invest that extra $40,000 in something that would bring them enough to offset the higher interest rate.

Since their monthly payments would be $434 per month

higher, they would be forced to get 13% interest on their "new" money in order to break even ($40,000 x 13% = $5,200 per year, or $433.33 per month).

This automatically ruled out all savings instruments available at that time from banks, savings and loans, brokerage houses, and insurance companies. None of them currently paid 13%. (If the interest on these savings instruments goes higher, mortgage rates will follow, and the spread will remain about the same.)

It also ruled out various U.S. government certificates and notes (as explained in Chapter 10). None of them currently yielded 13% either.

When they eliminate those types of investments, they move into the "riskier" classes. They could make more than 13% by buying contracts for deed or second mortgages, also explained in Chapter 10. The return on them can go as high as 20% to 30% or more, but the higher the return, the greater the risk of losing part or all of the investment.

They might get more than 13% by investing in common stock, but with higher risk. The current dividend rates of many stocks earn 9%, 10%, or even more, if their dividends and market prices stay the same, but the rest of the return has to come from stock appreciation. The price must go up enough to give Clarence and Elaine the extra 3% or 4% they need each year just to break even.

Yet another place to invest the $40,000 is to buy another piece of real estate. Buying a single-family dwelling might be a good investment, but only if inflation continues. They couldn't get enough in rent to cover the mortgage payments plus upkeep, much less give a 13% cash return on the down payment.

They might be able to buy a duplex or even a small apartment house, but the same holds true. Initial rental levels are seldom enough even to cover operation expenses. They will be in a few years if inflation continues, but in the meantime Clarence and Elaine may have to subsidize their newly acquired property out of their own pocket. Then their future is entirely dependent on inflation. If it comes under control or even slows, they could lose their extra property.

Clarence and Elaine had a real dilemma. They wanted to put some of their equity to work for them, but didn't know how to do it.

There is a way described in Chapter 10. In the meantime, their equity is working for them. It's providing them a place to live, financial security, and an excellent hedge against inflation. They don't really have to do anything.

We suggested that they first read Matthew 6:24, which says: "No one can serve two masters; for either he will hate the one and love the other, or he will be devoted to the one and despise the other. You cannot serve God and mammon" (RSV).

After getting back to serving "God first," they can look at their financial status much more maturely and objectively. God has given them a lovely home and all the furniture in it. He has made them trustees of three children and one good full-time job. Their responsibilities are to be good stewards of these trusts first.

It might be meaningful to look at how they can increase the wealth God entrusted to their temporary use if they would use that increase to serve him. So we'll look at their story later.

OLDER PEOPLE

Although retired people have more potential financial problems than any other age group, more has been done to help them alleviate these problems.

Senior citizen housing, for example, has taken in tens of

thousands of retired people all across the country. Rents are nominal for adequate and, in many cases, beautiful apartments. In some areas, seniors also get free maid service once a week, a luxury enjoyed by few working people.

Many retired people receive food stamps, substantially cutting the prices they pay for food; bus rides at reduced rates or even free; reduced real-estate taxes if they continue to live in their single-family homes; greatly reduced costs for medical care; fishing licenses; permits to use state parks; semi-automatic increases in social security and many other retirement benefits. In spite of these things, hundreds of thousands of seniors struggle financially and don't know from day to day where the money for their next meal is coming from.

Retired people also have the psychological problem of concluding that there is no room for them anymore. Many feel they are a burden on their families and give up trying to solve their problems.

Melanie Murphy wanted to continue to live in her family home after her children left and her husband died, but she had a problem. She was receiving social security, $350 a month, not enough to live on and keep up her house. While she was working, she had enough income to maintain the house in which she and her husband lived for 37 years before his death. With only social security and no pension from her former employers, there was no way she could pay the expenses on the house, plus food, clothing, and other necessities.

She thought about getting a part-time job, but to do that she would have to keep her car. The car expenses plus additional clothing and occasional lunches out would probably send her home each payday with a check smaller than the expenses incurred to get it.

She knew that if she sold her paid-up house, she would

receive a large amount of cash. She also knew that under a federal law, the large capital gain (difference between buying and selling prices) she would realize would be free from a capital gains tax that one time. So, selling the carefully maintained two-bedroom bungalow looked like the only possibility.

Melanie happened to live in Minnesota, one of the states that has a relatively new law permitting people to live on the equity in their homes. Because of the rapid increase in home values, people with small or nonexistent mortgages are permitted to receive monthly payments from a bank or savings and loan. In return, the bank or savings and loan has what amounts to a growing mortgage on the house. At the end of the loan period, Melanie could then sell her home and use the proceeds to pay off the loan. But she remembers the depression of the 1930s very well and doesn't like the idea of going into debt, regardless of the new conditions brought about by rapid inflation. After learning about this alternative, she decided not to use it, even though she admitted that "It might not be such a bad idea."

For Melanie Murphy, moving from her home, the neighbors, the lawn and garden that she loved so dearly, away from her church, the corner shopping area, and everything that meant so much, made it seem that life itself was almost coming to an end. She prayed about it, and her prayers were answered in a way that permitted her to stay in her home. The answer appears in Chapter 2.

Some retired people are confronted with other problems. How should they invest the money they have saved? Whom can they trust to help them with it? Should they make a will? Should they give away most of their assets before they die to make sure they go to the people they want to have them?

In investing cash surplus most retired people secure investments that will not fluctuate widely and that will send them a regular monthly check. Retired people are not trying to accumulate large quantities of money and property. They merely want a dependable and reliable monthly income so they can continue to live with comfort and security.

Second, they don't want to tie their money up in some investment where the money can't be withdrawn until two to four years later. They might have an emergency need, such as personal illness, a call for help from a family member, or a desire to give a gift, take a trip, or purchase something.

Obviously, if all of their money is in savings certificates which don't mature for 48 months, it is semi-tied up for that period of time. True, they can get it back in less than four years, but there would be a sharp drop in the rate of interest. They would have been better advised to put the money into some other kind of investment to get it when they want it, with no interest penalty.

Unless they are the rare retired persons with a large income, they probably will not want to invest in income property such as an apartment or commercial building. During a time of inflation, the prices of these buildings run ahead of their investment value, so the only way investors can break even is to hold them for several years until inflation raises rents to the level where they equal the costs of operation. In the meantime, investors have a "tax shelter" from the building through "depreciation allowance." But if they don't have a large income to shelter from federal and state income taxes, the tax advantage from income property is of little value. Besides, they may not want to wait several years for inflation—if, indeed, it does continue—to make their investment into a good one.

As retirees, you can do a number of things, depending

on your situation. You can invest in mutual funds for savers, really "money-market funds" under a variety of names. You put your savings into what amounts to a group savings-pool so it can be invested at the highest possible rate. We describe this more in Chapter 10.

Also available to you are 120-day, 10% (more or less) savings certificates, in denominations of $10,000 or more. The rate of return is excellent, and you get your money back in 120 days with no risk of loss.

If your particular problem, after reaching the age of retirement, is investments, you will probably follow this list of priorities.

1. **Liquidity:** you can get your money back in cash whenever you want it without penalty.

2. **Security:** little or no chance of your money being lost or frittered away in some declining investment.

3. **Yield, or rate of return:** the interest rate, or the yield on your investments is also very important in a time of inflation when you don't want to see your nest egg shrink by 10% or more every year.

4. **Opportunity for growth:** important even well after retirement, but less important than the first three priorities.

Another large expense for retired people is transportation, especially if they still own a car. Taxis for those necessary trips can add up, but buses are much cheaper if they are available and physically possible. Some senior-citizen programs help pay taxi fares.

If you still own a car, even though you drive it little, you'd probably be surprised at what it's costing you. Older people keep their cars much longer, so depreciation is not their major cost. But it costs $20 to $30 per month to rent a garage today. If you were not using your own, you could get good income by renting it to someone else.

Most repair shops charge between $25 and $30 per

hour to fix mechanical problems. It doesn't take long for $100 to disappear. Even that new $50 battery could be traded for ten $5 cab rides, or one hunded 50¢ bus rides.

There's more on the cost of car ownership and other types of transportation in Chapter 4.

Health care is another increasingly heavy financial burden for most retired people. In spite of Medicare, Medicaid, and all the other health programs, there are always insurance premiums, deductible fees, limits or uncovered items which creep in through what sometimes seem to be gaping holes.

When my mother broke her hip, only after she was taken to the hospital did we discover that neither Medicare nor her two "supplemental" insurance plans paid for ambulance rides. The bill was $168. Then there was the cost for an anesthesiologist of $126. We're still checking on this one, but it looks as if it's among the exclusions on this kind of surgery. That's $294 in unexpected expenses on those two items alone.

Then there are the illnesses and expensive hospitalizations that confront most retired people sooner or later. It is for this reason we urge all working people approaching retirement age to <u>make sure that any health insurance carried for them by their employers is transferable to an individual private policy that can be continued after they</u> retire. Because of the government programs, they may not want to continue the entire private insurance program. At the very least, they should carry any major-medical portion. Most of these major-medical portions start paying when hospital bills reach specific figures, such as $1000, $2000, or more. The government programs will pay much of the smaller amounts, so in either event, the sting of huge hospital and medical bills is not something you have to worry about. But you will have to be concerned with paying the premiums on the policy you have assumed from your former employer.

The time to plan for your health care is before you retire. Most group-insurance programs give you only a certain number of months in which to convert your employer's group to an individual program, owned and paid for by you. Plan it in advance, and you'll have the medical cost fear well in hand.

2

A Place to Live

> *Don't build your house and establish a home until your fields are ready, and you are sure that you can earn a living (Prov. 24:27).*

"Housing costs are out of sight," said the middle-aged woman, "and they seem to be going higher every day."

"We just can't afford to buy a house. The mortgage payments alone would be more than $600. Yet the cheapest apartment we can find costs $265 per month, and it's in a part of town where we wouldn't leave our car outside at night," said the newlyweds.

"We felt we could make it through our retirement years as apartment caretakers, but as the rents in the rest of the building have gone up sharply every year, the amount we've had to pay for our apartment, even with the work-allowance subtracted, has now gotten to the place we can no longer handle it. There's a long waiting list on the senior-citizen public housing and we just don't have the money to stay where we are. Besides, the work is getting too much for us anyway," said the 74-year-old retired couple. "What are we going to do?"

All of the above people concluded by saying, "But we need a place to live."

As a starter, there are at least a dozen alternatives. Each has advantages and disadvantages, but among them those who need a place to live can usually find an answer. Let's look at some, and see how inflation plays a role in the decision.

1. RENTING AN APARTMENT ALONE

If you are a couple or a single person, a rented apartment is usually the most economical place for you to live. It has several advantages.

First, you usually have some choice as to the part of town in which you live—but not always, as the rents may be too high in the areas you prefer.

Generally, you have some selection on the size of the apartment complex, size and layout of the apartment unit, and the rental lease. Some leases guarantee that your rent will not be increased for that period. Few other things which you will buy during the next 12 months carry the same guarantee. This is why many apartment owners are discarding the old 12-month lease requirement and substituting for it a straight 60-day notice. It means they can raise the rent more frequently if their costs rise rapidly.

But a shorter lease, or a 60-day notice, could be good news for you as well. It just might be that during that 12-month period something will happen to make it economically advisable for you to switch from renting an apartment to purchasing a condominium, mobile home, or even a single-family house.

Even a lease is seldom enforced. If the landlord wants to enforce it, the question becomes academic when apartments are in short supply. You can always find someone to take over the balance of your lease, providing it gives you the option of doing so. Make sure that option is in there when you first rent the apartment. It guarantees your freedom to leave when you want to.

Some apartment leases provide for automatic rental increases during the period of the lease. The landlord is probably paying more to heat the building, more for plumbing and electrical repairs, real-estate taxes, roof repairs, and all the rest. Money has to come from someplace, and the amount of rent you pay is that place.

When all is said and done, it is probably a good deal less expensive to rent an apartment than it is for you to buy and own your own home. The only place where you can come out ahead financially by owning a house, in most cases, is if inflation continues. Then the increased value of your house will eventually exceed the increased expense of owning it. But you can't "profit" from the inflation until you sell that house or borrow more money on it.

2. SHARING AN APARTMENT

Sharing an apartment does not work too well with married couples, although some are doing it. Splitting the cost of a two-bedroom apartment is increasingly common. As long as the apartment is large enough and the couples cause no trouble for other residents of the building, some landlords will permit it.

If you enter into this kind of agreement, make sure you and the other couple have *a written agreement* covering everything, including what is going to happen if one of you elects to leave. That agreement will probably provide that the mover will have the right to find another couple, or a single person, to take over your half of the lease for the balance of the period. Then make sure that the conditions on the acceptance of the individual are not so tight that it's impossible to find anyone to meet them.

It's amazing how close friends can suddenly become enemies where money is involved. Putting down all arrangements in writing, while you are still good friends, is the best way to avoid serious personal and legal problems.

Two or more single individuals living together has been common for years. It's an excellent financial arrangement and cuts normal rent in equal parts.

There are disadvantages to multiple occupancy. Who will buy the food? Who has the privilege of raiding the refrigerator and eating the food someone else has purchased? Are closets private for the person whose belongings are there, or can you wear each other's clothing? Such things should be talked out and put into writing in advance to guarantee a lasting and happy relationship. In addition, the termination or substitution arrangements should also be worked out in detail. If it's all down in writing, the relationship is more likely to be harmonious.

Finally, it's good to write a job description for each person to cover household chores. If not, one of the two will leave dirty dishes in the sink or wastebaskets full of refuse, and the other will end up providing free maid service.

3. RENTING A HOUSE ALONE

Renting a house is another option, but, unfortunately, most are available only on a temporary basis from people who have been transferred out of town or by people who are speculating. The latter have purchased the house as an investment and are hoping that inflation will raise the dollar value. In the meantime, it's available until they find a buyer at a profit.

This means that you, as the renter, have to ask for some kind of reasonable lease. Perhaps six months is the best you can do, but if it is acceptable to you, take it. At least you have that much time to find more permanent arrangements.

When leasing a home, it's important to know who is responsible for repairs and utilities. Many things may need doing or fixing. They range from fixing clogged toilets and sinks to watering and mowing the lawn and replacing broken windows.

As with any rental agreement, it's important to check the condition of the property before you move in and list all of the things you notice as being out of repair or damaged. If you don't, and if you don't get the agreement of the owner to your list of needed repairs, you may find yourself confronted with a long list of damages when it's time to leave.

In some instances you might rent a house, particularly a small one, for which the owner wants a caretaker. He wants someone to look after it more than he needs the income, and this could be a good short-term solution for both of you.

4. RENTING A HOUSE WITH SOMEONE ELSE

An increasingly attractive alternative is renting a house with someone else. Since houses are generally bigger than apartments, two individuals or couples have a greater opportunity for privacy, even though they live in the same house.

Again, most of the houses available for rental are on the market only for the short term. The most common sources today are speculators who have purchased single-family dwellings, hoping that inflation will help them get back more dollars than they put in. Most of these people are nervous investors and won't hold on to the houses forever. They are afraid of cycles in the market and don't have enough "staying power" to keep making the mortgage and upkeep payments on the house if inflation slows, rents decrease, or house prices drop. So be prepared for a relatively short stay.

You will find exceptions. Some people own several houses strictly as rental investments. They are generally smaller, inexpensive homes, because a rental home owner can't get enough rent to make his investment profitable if he buys a more expensive home.

Just as the main drawback is that you may be forced to move within six months to a year, the main advantage is that two or more people or couples can share the rent and other costs of upkeep. The cost per person is usually considerably less than renting an apartment or home on your own. Whenever a landlord permits it, four or five people sometimes get together and rent a house.

Shared housing has many possibilities. In Chapter 1 we told the story of Alice Olson and her three children. She is divorced, her earning power is limited, she can't afford to rent an apartment even if she can find one, and she doesn't want to live off welfare or in public housing. She's an ambitious, self-reliant person who wants to take care of herself and her own family and try to get ahead. All this on a limited income with heavy living expenses.

The first problem is finding housing. She won't accept public housing and welfare unless she becomes desperate. She has checked out regular apartment houses, and they reject her because of the three children or she has turned them down because of the cost.

She's looked at buying a house, but can't afford the down payment or the monthly payment. Finally, out of desperation, she's gone into the cheapest, most run-down areas of town, and discovered she can afford the housing, but feels that neither she nor the children would be safe outside, even in the daytime.

But there is at least one good alternative open to her.

Many other divorced women with children are looking for adequate housing; some of them managed to end up with the family house as a part of the divorce settlement. Many of them are also struggling financially and would welcome some help in carrying their financial loads.

Although it doesn't seem like a good option at first glance, more and more divorced women, particularly with children, will be looking at it closely in the years ahead. That option is to seek out another divorced woman with children and move in with her. Obviously, two families living together will create some problems. However, one of the problems that is greatly lessened is that of finances. If that hurdle can be overcome, the others can be worked out if the persons involved are determined to make it happen. It requires good discipline of the children, as well as of the parents, but the experience can be a rewarding and creative one as well as a realistic financial alternative.

Run an ad in the paper if you're in this position. Ask your friends, coworkers, relatives, fellow church-members, and everyone else you know.

Shared housing is also possible with widows, even those whose children are grown and away from home. Many homes are barely used with only one person occupying six or seven rooms. Many of these people would welcome help with finances in return for providing living quarters.

Obviously, if you have only one or two children, it will be easier to find this kind of situation than if you have six or eight. In any event, there are many possibilities in sharing homes. Because of economic necessity for both parties, it will be more common than it has been in the past.

Alice Olson will also probably be eligible for food stamps. This will help her reduce her cost of food and, even though it is a welfare program, it may be one that is acceptable to her. With the combination of moving into someone else's home and the use of food stamps, she will be able to make it while going through the period where her expenses are the highest and her earning power is starting to grow. The arrangement should be considered to be semi-permanent, and each day must be lived as it comes. Everything from remarriage to eventual financial improvement through a modest investment and self-improvement program (see Chapter 10) could eventually result in a change.

Melanie Murphy, whose plight was explained in Chapter 1, told her pastor she could no longer afford to keep her home. He had just been talking to another retired woman who was looking for housing. She couldn't afford to pay the $325 per month she had been quoted for a single-bedroom apartment, but had hoped to find a roommate to share the expense. The pastor introduced them, and before long they were discussing ways in which they could enjoy living together in Melanie's home.

The rent for the second woman was set at $200 per month, well below the cost for the apartment. In return, she would help with the housework; in fact, she looked forward to it. Their relationship was harmonious, and the renter soon learned that even though she had a free run of the house, whenever she was in her room, she had complete privacy.

The financial problem of these two single retired women was settled in a way that gave both of them several happy years of close friendship. But the time would come when Melanie Murphy would be physically unable to keep her house. At that time a relatively new tax law would help her.

Since her house had been hers for years, she knew it was worth many times what she paid for it. When she sold it, there would be a *capital gain,* which until mid-1978 would have been taxable as *capital gains income.* But in 1978 a federal law was passed which permitted a $100,000 once-per-lifetime capital gains exclusion on the sale of a personal residence. Here are the specific criteria that seller had to meet:

- The residence had to be sold after July 6, 1978.
- The residence had to be the taxpayer's principal residence.
- The taxpayer must have owned and used the residence for at least three of the last five years.
- The home owner must be at least 55 years old.
- The married couples who own a residence as joint tenants (meaning that if one of the two owners dies, the entire ownership reverts to the survivor), tenants by the entirety (meaning that if one of the two owners dies, his or her half of the property goes into his/her estate), or who live in community property states, and file a joint tax return, may get the $100,000 exemption if just one of them is 55 years or older. (And, of course, the other requirements are met.)

This exemption is available only once. If the exemption is used and the couple is subsequently divorced, no further exemption is available to either, or, if they remarry, to their new spouses. The same prohibition applies to widows and widowers who have used their exemptions. If they remarry, neither they nor their new spouses can get a further exclusion.

Melanie Murphy had the joy of living in her own home with a friend for company. She also knew that when the time came to sell, she would have financial security.

Shared housing could be the key to a happy home situation, and could be the only good alternative.

5. BUYING A SINGLE-FAMILY DWELLING

The most acceptable hedge against inflation and the most desirable housing goal for most people is buying a single-family home. As with everything else, it has advantages and disadvantages.

In the last few years, single-family dwellings have been appreciating in price faster than any other kind of real estate, including multiple dwellings. Consequently, a single-family dwelling is not only a good place to live, but an excellent hedge against inflation. If you put $10,000 down on a $60,000 home in 1977, in 1981 the home could be worth $85,000, and your equity will have increased from $10,000 to more than $30,000. In terms of purchasing power, the increase has been much less, but at least you would have kept pace with 10% per year inflation. Beside that, you've had a nice place to live.

But purchasing a single-family dwelling could be a far more expensive way to live than simply renting an apartment. No matter how much you want to buy a house before the price goes up, if you can't afford to make the payments, you'll lose it. Some people mistakenly put their faith in inflation to make them financially well again. Because of the many questions involved in home ownership and the fact that only 13% of the people can afford to buy a home today, we'll treat this subject in greater detail in Chapter 3.

6. BUYING A HOUSE YOU CAN'T AFFORD TO LIVE IN

If you have been faithfully setting aside 10% of your income from every paycheck (see Chapter 10) to build your savings nest egg, you will eventually have enough cash to make a down payment on a house. However, the

mortgage payments, along with interest, taxes and principal, plus upkeep, are likely to be so high that you can't
afford to live in it once it's yours.

If the house cost you $60,000, a $10,000 down payment
would leave you with a $50,000 mortgage. The principal,
interest, taxes, and insurance payments alone would
likely be in excess of $650 per month.

If you follow the rule of not spending more than 25%
of your pretax income for housing, you should be earning $2600 per month in order to afford such a house.
However, you may still be able to go ahead and buy a
house, if you don't move into it. The key is to stay in your
present housing. If you are a caretaker of an apartment
building and, therefore, having at least part if not all of
your apartment paid for through the labor you provide,
stay right where you are. Buy the house, after making
sure you can get enough rent for it to cover your out-of-
pocket expenses and payments.

It might be possible to get $650 per month rent for such
a house. This depends on the rental market in your area,
so you'll want to check it carefully before going ahead.
A good way is to check the want ads of houses for rent.
Then make the rounds to see how much the owners are
getting for houses of various sizes. Next, talk with real-
estate and rental management firms to learn how much
they are charging for rent. Once you understand the rental levels, and can get some assurance from a rental agent
or property manager that he can provide you with a tenant if you are not able to do it on your own, go ahead
and make the investment.

The worst that can happen is that you will be unable to
rent your house and have to move into it yourself. If that
happens, you will more than likely take in a roomer or
two to help you get enough income to carry the house
payments. The house will be so much larger than your

apartment that if you select your tenant carefully, it can be a satisfactory short-term relationship.

If you buy a house as an investment and rent it out, remember that it is not *homesteaded*. This means that since you don't live in it, you don't get the special lower real-estate tax category that you do when you live in the house. Consequently, the real-estate taxes will be a good deal higher. You also have a delay in taking off that higher tax. So, if you sell the house, the new owner will end up by paying the nonhomestead tax during his first year of occupancy because of the one-year delay in reassessing and reestablishing the homestead tax in most jurisdictions.

Check this option closely if you want to buy a house to beat inflation but can't afford to live in it.

7. BUYING A CONDOMINIUM

Buying a condominium is much the same as buying a house, except that your "house" is inside a larger building, and you are relieved of many upkeep chores.

You need to come up with a down payment, either assume the existing mortgage or take out a new mortgage, and make monthly mortgage payments (usually including your portion of the real-estate taxes) to the bank or savings-and-loan association.

In addition you pay a monthly or quarterly fee to the association that manages the building. Out of that fee come the payments for heating and air conditioning, the water used in the building and in maintaining the grounds, and all upkeep and maintenance. A part of it also goes to paying a building manager.

In a condominium, you agree to abide by the bylaws drawn up and accepted by the residents' association. Normally, the bylaws include the things you would want in order to have a pleasant place to live. So although they may be detailed, they are for your protection.

When the time comes to sell your condominium, if we are in an inflationary period and the price has gone up, you will benefit from that increased price. On the other hand, if a recession hits and the price goes down, you will lose accordingly.

Condominiums are becoming increasingly popular as more people want to get away from cutting a big lawn, shoveling snow, and worrying about everything from roof repairs to water heaters. Condominiums also have the advantage of permitting you to subtract the interest you pay on the mortgage from your income before paying federal income taxes and, in many cases, state income taxes.

The principal disadvantage is that condominium purchasing, like house purchasing, normally requires a significant down payment. If you buy a new unit, you might get in for a smaller amount, but then your monthly mortgage costs will be higher. The combination of the mortgage costs plus the monthly or quarterly maintenance fee could be out of your financial range.

As with purchasing a single-family dwelling, go through the same budget calculations and restrict yourself to the same spending limits. The U.S. Department of Housing and Urban Development, Washington, DC 20410, has an excellent pamphlet available, listing the things to look for in purchasing and selling a condominium.

8. BUYING INTO A CO-OP APARTMENT

When you buy into a co-operative apartment, you buy shares in an association. That association, in turn, owns the building. So, you don't actually own the apartment in which you live. The shares that you buy give you the right to live in one of the apartments and to participate in the operation of the building. In comparison, condominium buyers own and control their own apartments and have voting rights in the association that manages the common areas of the building.

If you want to buy into a co-op apartment, you will be required to pay the entry fee necessary to purchase shares of what amounts to stock in the co-op. These entry fees can be very high or sometimes quite low. They can be the smallest "down payment" you'll be able to make to acquire a permanent place of residence. In some areas they are as low as $2000 to $3000, but more commonly are at or above the $5000 level. So the "buy-in" price is not the chief advantage.

You also pay a monthly fee to the association, which covers all the costs of operating the building. In a way, it's like paying rent, but you have the advantage of a fee normally lower than rent would be. You also have the advantage of permanent residency and no danger of eviction, as long as you abide by the rules of the association.

The association is already paying on the building mortgage, so you have the benefit of what amounts to assuming a portion of the responsibility for that old, lower-interest-rate mortgage.

In addition, experience shows that when people own property, they take better care of it; consequently the building will be maintained better by the co-op owners than it would be if those same people were renting from a third party. As a result, monthly payments into the maintenance fund can be lower.

The association normally meets once a month to discuss the building and any problems. At those meetings you might decide to put on a new roof, even though you know it will mean an increase in your monthly payments; you might decide to replace the old furnace instead of repairing it; you very likely will become involved with such things as who gets the choice parking spaces, what to do about the noise from televisions late at night. You're a share-owner in a business, and that business is an apartment building.

One of the more common restrictions being written into some newly formed co-ops these days is that when you decide to leave, you cannot make a profit on your shares of stock, even though the value of the building might have doubled or tripled. You are required to sell them to a potential new owner for exactly what you paid, plus the amount that you have paid to lower the mortgage.

This approach is an effort to freeze the cost of housing near what it was on the day you purchased it, or if you're a second or third owner, on the day the co-op was formed. It's a good idea, even though it might not last forever. The members of the co-op association could, of course, vote to sell the building or could turn it into a condominium. If they did, they might realize a substantial profit, so the temptation will always be there.

In the meantime, however, co-op living seems to increase in popularity during times of tight housing. Co-ops are, generally speaking, one of the least expensive ways to live, and something worth looking into, even though there are few of them and, whenever a vacancy occurs, many buyers.

9. RENTING A MOBILE HOME

Another type of housing which is becoming increasingly popular is mobile homes. At one time they were eight feet wide and seldom more than 30 feet long. Today, those that are only 10 or 12 feet wide are considered to be narrow, since the widths go to 14 feet or more, and the lengths frequently exceed 60 to 70 feet.

In fact, some mobile homes have more square feet of living space than many permanent bungalows firmly anchored to concrete foundations.

In some areas mobile homes are available for rent in mobile-home parks. Owners of these parks often acquire extra mobile homes when owners move on and want to sell. The fastest and easiest way is to sell to the park owner, and little by little many of these park owners become owners of extra homes.

If you are looking for a relatively inexpensive and relatively comfortable place to live, check out the mobile-home parks in your area. You can have the same leasing arrangement as with apartments, but check on the inconveniences as well as the conveniences. Make sure the mobile home is well mounted and insulated, particularly so that the water lines won't freeze. Make sure, also, that bottled liquid petroleum (LP) gas is available in the area, and find out who pays for it and how much it might cost in addition to the rent.

Work out your entire 12-month housing budget, even including the dimes and quarters for those coin-operated washing machines. Then you won't have any unpleasant surprises later on.

10. PURCHASING A MOBILE HOME

Like most new cars, mobile homes depreciate in value, even though during inflationary times they are holding their value much better. You will find them for sale in almost every mobile-home park. But before buying one, familiarize yourself with the mobile-home market. One way is to ask dealers what they have for sale and what they offer in prices and conditions. Dealers know where the money can come from to get the mortgage you will probably need. On the other hand, a private owner may already have a good mortgage, which might be transfer-able.

Some banks and lending institutions are reluctant to finance mobile homes if the loan is applied for by the pur-chaser. One reason is that most mobile-home loans run for about 12 years, and during that period of time a mo-bile home will generally decrease in value. Inflation may help it hold its value, but usually does not increase it. Consequently, when the loan gets to be several years old, the balance due may exceed the market value.

Another reason for this reluctance is that the maximum legal interest rate that can be charged for mobile-home loans in a direct loan from a bank to a purchaser may be lower than the prime interest rate. The prime rate was above 20% in early 1980 and most commercial loans were being written at 20% to 22%, but mobile home loans, where available, were about 15%. It's obvious that banks can get a much better rate of return on their investments by making commercial or business loans. Furthermore, commercial loans are generally made for much shorter periods of time, giving the bank an opportunity to then reinvest its money at higher interest rates, if they change during that period.

However, you can finance mobile homes through a dealer, if you buy from him. In this way, you purchase on what is called a "conditional sales contract," which means the title stays with the dealer until you make your final payment. These "three-name" loans, which carry the names of the dealer, the bank, and yours, can carry a higher interest, usually 1% to 2% above the prime rate. In this way they are acceptable to the banks and can result in the loan being approved.

Such an arrangement, of course, will have higher monthly payments. So shop around for your loan. Some banks will make mobile-home loans for a full 12-year period, even if your state does have a statutory limit on the amount of interest they can charge on such loans.

It's just as important to find a place to park your mobile home as it is to find and finance it. If it's already up on blocks, well installed, and insulated underneath, you'll save over buying a new one and then having to pay several hundred dollars for it to be towed to a mobile home park and set up. That's an expensive proposition not often fully explained by the salesman.

My recommendation is that if you like the idea of a mobile home and it fits into your budget, purchase a used model, one already well set up on a convenient park, and one that has a lease with the park owner that guarantees you the present monthly land rental costs for at least several months. Like rent for apartments, rent for these parking spaces is going up every year.

If you buy a mobile home that is already set up, make sure the lease is transferable, and that there is no way the park owner can force you to move. If he does, it may cost you dearly. It's expensive to move something that is 14 feet wide and 76 feet long, especially when you discover that you may not have purchased the wheels and axle along with it.

Some leases are drawn heavily in favor of the park owner and are one reason many home owners sell their mobile homes to the park owner when they move. Nobody else will buy them because they cannot leave them where they are sitting unless the mobile park owner agrees to the sale (sometimes at a substantial "lease transfer fee"). The owners are then left with no alternative but to sell to the person who owns the park. You can guess that the price will be low.

On the other hand, there is a definite increase in the popularity of mobile homes as a desirable place to live. Many are well constructed, are large and comfortable, and cost much less than the same square footage of permanent housing.

Some people have combined the best of a permanent home and a mobile home. They've bought a lot, maybe at a lake, then checked all the local zoning regulations for the area. After purchasing the mobile home to park on their lot, they have the security of owning the land plus having the lower housing costs from owning the mobile home. They may end up with a little more gasoline costs to get back and forth to work, but if you figure your costs carefully, you might find it's the best for you.

11. MANAGING AN APARTMENT BUILDING

Managing apartment buildings is another excellent possibility for housing, particularly for couples where one person is unemployed. Apartment owners and renters like to have couples as resident managers or caretakers because they want to have someone at the building most of the time. The managers are there to let repairmen in to fix the furnace or the plumbing, or somebody's dishwasher or garbage disposal. At times tenants will inadvertently lock themselves out of their own apartments and will want someone to let them back in.

In return for your willingness to look after the building, mow the lawns, shovel the sidewalk, rent apartments, and perform minor maintenance, you'll normally get a free apartment. In the larger buildings, you'll get a modest salary on top of the apartment, and in the smaller buildings, you'll get a reduction in the monthly rent.

Many young couples and retired couples have found this to be their best way of securing affordable housing. It's one way to have a part-time job, and still be at home while you are working.

Some people have made a full-time career out of being

resident apartment managers. To do so, they have to find larger complexes, usually 60 to 70 units or more. These complexes are big enough to provide a free apartment for the caretaker, plus a salary. The larger the number of units, of course, the larger the salary.

Another opportunity for couples is to be caretakers in a large apartment complex, which also has a resident manager. The manager runs the project, and handles the rentals and bookwork. The resident caretaker does the work of mowing the lawn, shoveling snow, cleaning the swimming pool, and other maintenance. Such an arrangement works well for a young couple when both husband and wife are working. They need not be at the building all day to take care of the repairmen or show vacant units; the resident managers will take care of those things. The caretakers do most of the physical work and can handle it in the evenings and on weekends. It's an excellent arrangement for couples who are willing to roll up their sleeves and dig in. Then, with the money they are saving from the rent, they can start building their own savings toward the day when they buy their own home or multiple dwelling.

12. SHORT-TERM ACCOMMODATIONS

Some people like to have someone live in their homes (including apartments) while they are away on extended vacation. Sometimes these vacations run for six months out of the year. The rent they charge could be minimal, as the main thing they are interested in is the security of their homes. If you are interested in this, have good references to show you are the kind of trustworthy people with whom the owners can leave their home and all of its valuable contents.

Another relatively short-term arrangement could be to

rent a lake cottage. Many people own lake homes which they use for only two or three weeks out of the year. The rest of the time they are vacant.

If you happen to live in an area with many of these cottages, you might be able to work out cottage-sitting arrangements. You'll end up by mowing the lawn, making sure it isn't burglarized, and generally keeping it up just as if it were your own. In return you won't have to buy furniture and may not have to pay more than minimum rent.

You will have to be prepared to move out whenever the owners want to come in for their annual vacation. You might also find that the cottage may not be suitable for year-round occupancy, and you can live in it only from about the first of April until the end of October, minus the month or more that the owners want to occupy it themselves. But with a little searching it's an arrangement that might fit your needs.

Inflation plays a definite role in your planning for your housing, regardless of your age or your economic status, but God helps his children in this vital area of living as he does in others. Christians can depend on God to take care of them in their housing needs. Prayer and faith in God are two ingredients that will help you in this matter of housing.

3

Buying a Home

> If one of you is planning to build a
> tower, he sits down first and fig-
> ures out what it will cost, to see
> if he has enough money to finish
> the job. If he doesn't, he will not
> be able to finish the tower after
> laying the foundation; and all who
> see what happened will make fun
> of him (Luke 14:28-29).

In the previous chapter, we pointed out that even
though owning a house is one of the best ways of staying
even with inflation, the rapid increase in cost has put
homeowning out of reach of most people. Even knowing that, it is still perfectly normal for you to want to
achieve this American dream. So let's look at it a little
more carefully.

In 1980 the average price of a single-family dwelling
rose to $62,000 and in some areas, like San Francisco,
to more than $100,000.

The average home in most larger metropolitan areas
in 1980 cost $70,000. In the early 1980s, according to
many economists, the rest of the country will have

reached California's level. And California will more than likely continue to increase.

This means that if you live in the San Francisco Bay area and want to purchase a basic three-bedroom house, and if you follow the old rule of not paying more than twice your annual before-tax earnings for a home, you would have to earn $50,000 per year to buy that house. Since few individuals have reached that salary level, both husband and wife must have full-time jobs, and well-paying ones at that, to be able to purchase this home.

This is why the experts predict that even a smaller percentage of American families will be able to afford a home of their own. One bank in California reported that more than 50% of their mortgage loans are now made to two-income households, up from 30% five years ago.

When house prices reach the point that even fewer families can afford them, a series of economic forces will move into action to bring houses within the reach of more people again. New methods of construction, cheaper financing, a leveling of house prices, or other factors will come into the picture. If houses remain out of reach indefinitely, the percentage of people who can afford to buy homes will continue to drop almost to zero. At that point, those who are forced to sell their homes because of necessary moves, debts, or personal reasons will have to cut prices to bring them within reach of the remaining buyers. But the long-range trend of prices for houses in terms of current U.S. dollars will likely continue upward.

BUYING A HOUSE YOU CAN AFFORD

If you were able to buy that average priced $62,000 home with an FHA loan, with $3000 cash (including approximately $1000 for closing costs), you would end up with a $60,000 mortgage. To simplify things, if you could get a $60,000 mortgage loan carrying 12% interest, the interest alone would be $7200 per year, or $600 a month. Add to that a small amount for payments on the principal, plus insurance and taxes, and the minimum cost of living in your $62,000 home would probably be over $800 per month.

If you can come up with $13,000 to cover the down payment and the $1000 closing costs on this $62,000 home, you'd carry "only" a $50,000 mortgage. At the 12% interest rate that brings the annual interest down to $6000, or $500 per month. But you still have taxes, insurance, and payment on the principal, so your net 'out-of-pocket monthly payments will be about $700, still a large outlay for housing, not even counting utilities and upkeep.

In 1980 you could rent a nice apartment in most areas for about half the cost of your house. The only offsetting advantage of buying the house is inflation, the reason many are urging buying a house before prices go up. But if you can't afford to make the monthly payments on the house, you will lose it. You are faced with some tough choices.

According to the May 28, 1979 issue of *U.S. News and World Report,* in the first quarter of 1978 22.7% of the average consumer's paycheck went to paying off interest and principal on loans, other than for real-estate mortgages. That was up from 19.6% in the third quarter of 1975, and by early 1980 it's undoubtedly higher.

According to a good rule of thumb, not more than 25% of your pretax income should go toward making mortgage principal and interest house payments. This means that if your payments are $750 per month, you should have an income of $3000 per month before taxes to afford a house with payments of that size.

Another rule of thumb says you should not buy a house for a price more than double your annual pretax income. If you earn $30,000 per year before taxes, you can afford to buy a $60,000 house. Some financial experts say you should not pay more than 1.8 times your annual pretax income. Under this tougher guideline, the $30,000 person could pay only $54,000 for a house. You can see how this narrows the market and makes it almost impossible for most couples with even two incomes to afford a house, unless they get help from their parents or others.

The U.S. Department of Housing and Urban Development estimates that in 1970 half of the families in the United States could afford to buy a medium-priced house —then $23,400—by the 25% payment rule. In 1980, by that standard, only 13% could afford new-home ownership.

THE TWO-INCOME FAMILY

If you are a two-income family to get to these levels, and you suddenly lost one of those incomes, you could be in trouble. An even safer rule is to base the value of the house you can afford on the income of one wage earner who is likely to be permanently employed.

An exception to this rule is having a considerably larger down payment on the house. You may have built up your equity through a series of homes you have owned and are now able to move up in the size and cost of your house. Referring to an illustration used earlier, if you bought that $62,000 home with a $33,000 down payment, your mortgage would be $30,000. The annual interest at 12% is $3600, or $300 per month; with the principal, taxes, and insurance your total payment is nearly $500 per month, or $6000 per year. The 25% rule means that your income should be at least $24,000 per year before taxes, but because of the larger down payment you have been able to get a house worth much more than the $48,000 allowed under the "two-times" earnings rule.

Thirty-eight percent of all buyers ignore that prudent rule, but they pay a big price by working two jobs, forcing both husband and wife to have jobs, going without many other things, and frequently wondering where the next payment is coming from. In 1980 almost half of all home buyers were families with two incomes.

In 1948, according to the National Women's Political Caucus, only about 12% of all mothers with school-age children were in the work force. In 1980 43.7% of those mothers were working, an amazing increase of 350% and still rising steadily. Experts predict that by 1990 only 25% of American wives and mothers will be staying home full time with their children.

This trend toward working mothers, particularly those with young children, is already having tragic results. Several studies reveal that working women have a significantly higher divorce rate than those who stay at home.

Having both husband and wife working to help buy a new house is all right until children are born. If it is then necessary for the mother to continue working to make house payments, the price is too high to justify home ownership. Besides, the net amount brought home by the working mother is much smaller than it appears to be. Consider these items: a higher tax bracket caused by two salaries, her extra clothes, charges for babysitting, extra lunches, extra cost of instant food (used because the parents don't have time to prepare other meals), transportation, possibly extra doctor bills, sometimes the problem of added conflict over money ownership. Does the wife's money belong to her? Does the husband's money belong to him? Or does the combined amount belong to both of them? And if so, what if the husband wants to buy a set of golf clubs, or take a fishing trip, and the wife thinks she has earned the extra money and feels it should go for something in the home?

Apart from finances, other problems arise. Some psychologists tell us that a working wife deflates her husband's ego and that men need to be admired. Is it God's best plan that children be reared by babysitters? Increased pressure causes more health problems and increases the possibility of husband and wife becoming attracted to others.

For working parents, there is also the additional question of day care for their children. The average cost of full-time child care in a licensed family day-care home or day-care center was between $1800 and $3000 per child per year in 1980, more than many middle-income families can afford to pay. A good share of that second salary, therefore, will not be available to help pay for the house.

From the financial standpoint alone, a careful calculation of all of the financial factors shows that a working mother adds very little *net* income to the family treasury.

FINDING MONEY FOR A HOME

A study made by the Joint Center of Urban Studies of the Massachusetts Institute of Technology and Harvard University in 1977 concluded that 46% of America's families could afford to purchase a home in 1970, but six years later, in 1976, only 27% could afford a median priced home. The National Association of Home Builders in 1980 estimated that only 9% of American families had income sufficient to qualify for the purchase of a median-priced new single-family home.

This means that even though a home is an excellent investment and an excellent hedge against inflation, the great majority simply can't afford to make the monthly payments and have anything left for food, clothing, transportation, and upkeep on the house. You may need to give serious thought to long-range alternatives, even if it means shelving a lifelong dream of house-ownership for the next few years.

There are exceptions, of course. If you put a higher value on a house than on transportation and recreation, you can decide to go without a car. You can also decide that your vacations for the next few years can be spent at home, painting it, working in the yard, and visiting local places of interest. If your priorities put the ownership of a home above most other things, you might be able to commit 30% of your pretax income into paying for your house.

As you juggle the other costs of living and establish your own list of what's most important, you can decide what percentage of your income you want to spend on housing. But remember, it's tough to put 30% of your pretax income into housing. So, if you decide to commit that much, you will have to tighten your belt even more. Still some people can do it because of their strong desire for a home of their own.

But as Christians we should beware of being obsessed with possessions; Jesus warned, "Watch out and guard yourselves from every kind of greed; because a person's true life is not made up of the things he owns, no matter how rich he may be" (Luke 12:15). A Christian may need to have other priorities than paying an above-average amount for a house.

Other factors might make a house purchase a little easier. For example, you may find a home for sale which has an older mortgage, which is transferable to the new buyer, with interest rates of 7%, 8%, or 9%, well below the 1980 interest rates of 12% or higher.

Another important point to remember is that loans guaranteed by the Veterans Administration and the Federal Housing Administration can be assumed, and the initial rate for VA loans cannot be increased. But there is a big drawback: the seller must be paid the difference between the selling price and the balance owed on his mortgage, which often is large because of the rise in home values in recent years.

It may be that in the near future, all old mortgages will be assumable by new buyers, just as is now true for all FHA and VA guaranteed loans. For years many lenders have inserted clauses in mortgage agreements that prevent the automatic assumption of old mortgages by new buyers. However, in a 1979 case in California the State Supreme Court ruled that a new buyer could assume an existing mortgage at the old interest rate and didn't have to comply with the bank's requirement of a new mortgage at a higher rate.

As of January 1980, courts in eight other states have made similar rulings; these states are Alaska, Alabama, Arizona, Florida, Michigan, Mssissippi, New Mexico, and Oklahoma. More states are expected to follow. Some loans might be excluded from state rulings, so it might be best to check with your local lender or realtor.

Older low-interest mortgages are usually small, and the seller normally has a big equity. He or she may want to cash out that equity, but might carry a contract for deed or second mortgage for part of it. This secondary financing, which may run directly to the person from whom you bought the home, can usually be negotiated at an interest rate lower than the current rate banks and saving-and-loan associations are charging for their mortgages. You might even end up with one at 8% on top of an old 7% mortgage.

If you buy a $62,000 house, plus the $1000 closing costs,

and have only $3000 down, you may assume the old $30,000 mortgage balance at 7% and take a new $30,000 contract for deed or second mortgage at 8%. Then your average rate of interest is only 7¹/₂%, and although you have two payments to make each month, the interest is only $375 a month, rather than the $600 (at 12%), or more, that you would pay with an FHA or conventional loan. It's a substantial saving.

The main disadvantage to you is that the secondary financing will have what is called a "balloon" at its expiration date. This means, that at some future time, usually not more than seven years, you will be required to come up with the cash to pay off the full balance.

After seven years you may have paid the $30,000 contract for deed or second mortgage down to $23,200, so you will need to come up with $23,200 cash. At the same time, you will have paid the $30,000 mortgage down to a somewhat lower figure, perhaps $26,500.

If nothing else is available, at this point you can usually go to a bank or other lending institution and borrow $23,200 on a regular commercial second mortgage for your home. This is becoming more and more of a common financing method as inflation increases the market value of homes. Although you must plan for the balloon payment, there will be money available to pay it, at a higher interest rate, assuming inflation continues. But even if inflation doesn't continue and your house price stays exactly the same, barring major recession, you can still get money to pay off that second mortgage when it comes due.

In the meantime, if you've been frugal in your living and have built up a new cash reserve, that can be applied on the secondary financing; the amount you need to borrow to make the balloon payment will be less.

Another danger in having a second mortgage or a contract for deed in addition to the original mortgage is the problem of missing payments. State laws vary on such things as delinquencies and foreclosures. But it is common to permit a buyer to stay in a house for at least six months, and sometimes as long as 12 months, even though no mortgage payments were made during that period of time. Foreclosure proceedings would be started by the lending institution during that period, but you as the delinquent buyer could not be evicted sooner.

If you borrow money on a contract for deed or a second mortgage—again depending on your state laws—the lender may be able to force you out of the house when you become 30 to 60 days delinquent in making any payment. If you do use a contract for deed or second mortgage to fill the gap between the low interest rate first mortgage and your down payment, read it carefully and then budget carefully so you can comply with its terms.

Another saving when buying instead of renting is that the interest you pay on the mortgage is deductible from your income before you pay federal and state taxes. If the interest rate is 11%, depending on your tax bracket, the "effective" interest you are paying could be only 7% or 8%.

If worse comes to worse, you can always sell the house. Unless the economy collapses, you will at least get back your down payment plus the equity you have built up through reducing the mortgage and contract for deed, minus any sales fee.

Because changing market conditions make some advice obsolete rather quickly, it's always good to seek current knowledgeable advice on all aspects of home purchasing, ownership, and sale. Your realtor and banker will be happy to give you that advice.

ADDITIONAL SUGGESTIONS

1. When you look for your first house, try the older sections of town. Although they may seem to be run-down, neighborhoods go through phases. These range from excellent to mediocre to poor, then into rehabilitation and back into being an excellent place to live.

If you can find a home in an old district bordering on a college or university, you are likely to find your neighborhood getting special attention. In the meantime, the value of the land on which your house sits is probably growing even faster than the house itself.

Purchasing an older home needing repairs you can make yourself is one way to get into real-estate ownership without paying what the same square footage would cost in a new neighborhood or suburban area.

2. Buying a home with someone else, even a single family dwelling, is another alternative and a hedge against inflation.

Such a shared purchase arrangement is even more common on double bungalows or duplexes. Usually the price of a double house is less than the price of two single homes, yet the living is just as comfortable. The purchase price may not make it attractive as a pure investment, since the rent from both halves may not even cover expenses, but such a joint venture may make your monthly expenses and mortgage payments affordable.

3. It is traditional to recommend that a buyer secure as large a mortgage as possible, running as long as possible, to keep the down payment as small as possible. One reasoning for this is that if you must sell your house in the relatively near future, you will have an easier time finding buyers if only a small down payment and small monthly payments are required. In addition, there was a time when you could easily invest any extra cash in investments

that paid more than the interest rate you were paying for your mortgage. It is still good to get the longest terms possible (30 years is better than 25), but this recommendation regarding down payments is no longer necessarily sound.

During a time of extremely high mortgage interest rates, it may be desirable to make as much of a down payment on a house as you can afford, always holding back enough cash for the many expenses related to moving into and equipping your new home. This advice is the opposite of what it was before inflation took such a strong grip on our country. Then you could earn more interest elsewhere. But with mortgage rates running frequently above 12%, when you make a large down payment you are, in effect, getting 12% interest on your money. Few investments yield the average person a guaranteed higher return. If you make a minimal down payment and keep the balance of your money in a passbook savings account, for example, you get only about $5^1/2\%$ return.

Keep enough cash on hand for emergencies and operating, but recognize that the interest on the mortgage is probably the highest return you can get. In a high interest-rate period pay as much down as possible, try to get the longest possible payback period. It's also likely that if inflation continues and the value of the dollar declines, you will be paying your long-term mortgage with "cheaper" dollars. That's good.

4. After you have purchased a house, and after you have rebuilt your operating or living reserve, for most people it is a good idea in a high interest-rate economy to pay that mortgage off as fast as reasonably possible, but only as long as the interest rate on the mortgage is higher than you could earn elsewhere. Make sure your mortgage allows you to pay additional amounts without penalty.

5. Many ways are available to you to finance the purchase of a home. A good real-estate agent can give you the details on all of them. But here is a list, merely to indicate the variety of possible avenues open to you.

- Cash
- Trade (almost anything)
- Assumption of existing mortgage
- A new conventional mortgage
- A GI mortgage
- An FHA mortgage
- A contract for deed or second mortgage
- FHA loan for veterans
- A special FHA-245 graduated payments mortgage (payments smaller in earlier years and gradually getting larger)
- Refinancing other property
- Low-interest loans from government subsidy programs
- Combination of cash, assumption of existing mortgage, and contract for deed
- Wrap-around contract (You pay previous owner; he keeps part and makes original mortgage payments).
- Corporation financing provided by your employer

6. Low-interest loans from public agencies are periodically available in some parts of the country. The public agencies can be either state or local, and they are in the home-purchase-and-improvement financing business. These agencies get their money by selling tax-exempt bonds to the public, and then lending the money to citizens who meet their basic qualifications.

To qualify for such a loan in 1979, your income had to be under $16,000, the amount of the loan could not exceed $37,500, and the interest rate in at least one metropolitan area was $6\frac{3}{4}\%$, far below the regular commercial mortgage or home-improvement interest rates.

Other requirements exist as well, but most of them are easily met by present or potential owner-occupants of single-family dwellings and even multiple dwellings or condominiums in some cases.

This is, however, not a reliable or significant source of funds. The amount of money that can be raised by these various state or local government agencies through the sale of bonds is sharply limited. This means that whenever they do sell some bonds and have money available, long lines of applicants appear, and the money runs out before even a small percentage of the applicants receive any.

7. Buying and selling houses to make money, or buying houses to rent out as investments, has many angles. Federal law permits you to sell one house one time and keep the capital gain (up to $100,000, and if you are at least 55 years old and have lived in the house at least three of the last five years), which is the difference between the price you pay for it and the price you get for it. If you do sell more than one house, your tax rate on the second capital gain is your normal income tax rate applied to 40% of the gain. More on this in Chapter 12.

8. Make sure you're getting interest on tax escrow deposits. For many years some buyers received no interest on their money which lending institutions were collecting monthly to make semiannual real-estate tax payments. The lenders maintained that the expense of keeping the records on that money and then paying the taxes for the owner more than offset the interest they earned by investing the tax money while they held it.

In recent years several states, either through laws, court cases, or out-of-court settlements, have adopted procedures requiring lenders to pay interest, or to make other concessions on mortgage escrow funds. These states are California, New York, Illinois, Washington, Texas, Pennsylvania, and under certain conditions, Oregon. In early 1979 suits were pending in Virginia, North Carolina, and Maryland, where groups were seeking interest on their tax escrow funds (*Wall Street Journal,* July 23, 1979). Your state may already require lending institutions to pay you interest on your accumulated tax funds before they are paid out to the real estate tax collecting authority (usually your county or municipality or taxing district). This is a relatively small income item, but one you should also take into consideration when you are preparing a razor-thin home-owning budget.

9. Purchase your home from the Veterans Administration. Each year the VA takes back thousands of homes on which they had guaranteed the mortgage, but the buyers defaulted. They are usually lower priced, require a smaller down payment, and have mortgages ready to go. Call your local VA office for details.

10. When the VA or FHA insures home mortgages, you can buy a house for a lower down payment because the lender can always collect from the "insurer." However, FHA loans (requiring down payments of 3% of the first $25,000 in value and 5% of the remainder) are limited to mortgages of $67,500. If you can afford a more expensive property, you can get it with a smaller down payment if you purchase mortgage insurance through one of the 14 or 15 American companies offering it. When the average priced home is now over $70,000, if your budget allows the payments, this private insurance will help get you the mortgage you need.

Purchasing a home is about the safest investment anyone can make, especially in a time of inflation. Just make sure you can handle the payments, the upkeep, utility bills, routine maintenance, and unexpected but necessary repairs. Also remember that as a Christian you acknowledge that everything in the world belongs to God. We may possess things, but God owns them. The psalmist wrote, "The world and all that is in it are his" (Psalm 24:1).

Once we recognize God's ownership of everything we possess, it relieves us of a certain amount of responsibility. We're still responsible to be good managers of the property and resources he has put in our trust, but it is God's responsibility to take care of that property. If you believe God wants you to be a steward of one of his houses, home ownership might be a wise move for you.

THE SIZE OF MORTGAGE YOU CAN CARRY

The estimates are for monthly principal and interest payments on a 30-year mortgage. Calculate all your other living expenses, subtract them from your income, and what is left will be the amount you can afford for housing—including mortgage payments.

Loan Amount	10%	10½ %	11%	11½ %	12%	12½ %	13%	13½ %	14%
$20,000	$176	$183	$190	$198	$206	$213	$221	$229	$237
$25,000	219	229	238	248	257	267	277	286	296
$30,000	263	274	286	297	309	320	332	344	355
$35,000	307	320	333	347	360	374	387	401	415
$40,000	351	366	381	396	411	427	442	458	474
$45,000	395	412	429	446	463	480	498	515	533
$50,000	439	457	476	495	514	534	553	573	592
$55,000	483	503	524	545	566	587	608	630	662
$60,000	527	549	571	594	617	640	664	687	711
$65,000	570	595	619	644	669	694	719	745	770
$70,000	614	640	667	693	720	747	774	802	829
$75,000	658	686	714	743	771	800	830	859	889

4

Providing Transportation

> *Get the facts at any price and hold on tightly to all the good sense you can get (Prov. 23:23).*

How would you like to pay $8 per gallon for gasoline? In at least one country people paid that much in 1980. Even in the United States in 1980 the cost of transportation, for some people, already exceeded the cost of food. The only higher living expense is usually housing, and for some, even that is less. In a time of inflation, with the margin between income and expenses getting smaller every payday, it makes sense to look carefully at how much we are spending on transportation.

In 1979 the cost of gasoline increased by about 100%, from approximately 50¢ a gallon to more than $1 a gallon. This is still a long way from the $2.50 to $3 price common in the rest of the world. We are heading higher and can expect gasoline to be $2 per gallon or more in the future.

The one-dollar figure caused only a minor change in driving habits. We drove almost as much as when gasoline was 50¢, or even 30¢, a gallon.

One problem is that we don't really admit how much it costs us to drive our cars. These costs are rising steadily, but a 1979 study by the American Automobile Association shows that a subcompact, in low-cost areas (small towns and rural locations) starts at 14.8¢ per mile. In high-cost areas (large metropolitan areas), costs start at 18.4¢ per mile.

Based on driving 15,000 miles annually, medium-size cars cost 19.7¢ per mile to operate in low-cost areas, and 24.6¢ in high-cost areas. The Hertz Corporation, a large renter and leaser of cars, reported in early 1980 that it now costs 38¢ per mile, up 5¢ per mile in one year, to operate a medium-sized sedan driven 10,000 miles per year and owned three years. Your cost per mile could be even higher if you have an air conditioner, if you make fast starts and stops, and if you are careless in your maintenance. These figures are on the high side, principally because the Hertz organization operates new cars with a heavier depreciation than would be realized from buying and operating secondhand cars.

Translating these per-mile costs into daily costs helps us understand the enormous expense of owning and operating an automobile. If you are driving a standard-size car in a metropolitan area on a 30-mile round trip to work, it's costing you $9 per day (using a compromise 30¢ per mile figure)—not counting parking charges. That's $45 per week, a substantial outlay that does not include all your other weekly miles.

These costs are based on driving cars less than three years old. If you drive a used car and bought it as a secondhand vehicle (which I recommend), your cost per mile could and should be significantly lower. But it's still high.

Even when people discover how much it costs to drive, some keep right on driving. To make up the difference, they stop eating lunch out, or they find some other way to conserve in order to have the luxury of driving the car whenever they want.

SOME PRACTICAL COST-CUTTERS

We can still hold on to our automobiles and actually reduce our cost of transportation at a time when cars, gasoline, service, and everything that goes with them is increasing in price.

1. Some are moving closer to their jobs. At one time it was not uncommon to live on the far north side of town and work on the far south side, and drive 20, 30, or 40 miles a day. More people are looking for apartments or homes much closer to work. This makes sense, particularly if they are long-term employees and relatively certain of permanent employment.

2. Some are looking for new jobs closer to home. If it's hard to move because your husband or wife has a job near the home where you presently live, the kids are in school, and your church is just around the corner, you might want to consider quitting your present job after you have found a new one nearby. Sometimes this is not possible or desirable, and at other times it is possible only at a reduced salary. But that lower salary may increase, and perhaps even at the start you'll break even because you no longer have the long daily drive.

3. Some are reducing transportation costs by choosing a church closer to home. This may be difficult, particularly if you've grown up, been baptized, attended Sunday school, and been a key part of a distant church. However, the trend toward attending neighborhood churches is likely to accelerate. Even though I was raised in a downtown church, was active in many of its programs, and loved it dearly, when we moved into a residential neighborhood and realized that our children would be going to church two and three times every week, we transferred to one nearby. Since then, all three children have completed weekly confirmation classes, sung weekly in our young

people's choir, been active in the teen group, and we ourselves have attended many meetings at church. Being able
to walk to church has saved hundreds of gallons of gasoline per year. That's extra money we can give to the work
of the Lord. Beside that, we have also saved many hours of
driving.

4. Many are discovering they no longer have to run to
the grocery store to get a quart of milk. All they need do
is plan a little better, and they can combine all shopping
into one trip per week. Just a minor change in life-style
does it.

5. People are also discovering ways to get more miles
out of every gallon of gasoline. For example, experts have
discovered that efficient air conditioners can save gasoline
at speeds of 40 mph or more, because the wind drag from
open windows burns more fuel than does the cooling.

Warming up your engine before driving burns gasoline
unnecessarily, and warming it for just a few minutes does
no good, since it takes about 20 minutes to reach maximum efficiency through operating heat. It's much better
to let the engine idle about 30 seconds or so and then
drive off, warming up on the way.

Remove unnecessary weight from your car. Lightening
it by 100 pounds will provide up to an extra half mile per
gallon.

Short trips are fuel wasters. Trips of five miles or less
account for about 15% of the mileage on American cars,
but consume more than 30% of the gasoline. The reason
is that the trip is over before the engine begins to operate
at peak efficiency, which comes when the engine is fully
warmed up after about 20 minutes of driving.

Avoid jackrabbit starts, but try to get up to the best
mileage range of 40-50 mph reasonably fast. Avoid accel-
erating while going up hills. Avoid high-speed driving
directly into strong winds. Stay within the speed limit. All

these are ways of increasing miles per gallon. Gasoline consumption savings can be dramatic. By following these tips, most drivers manage to save between 20% and 40%, and some as much as 48%. This means that the good drivers can cut their gasoline consumption almost in half while still driving as many miles as before, and even the average driver with minimum effort can cut fuel consumption by as much as 10% without the slightest inconvenience or sacrifice.

SOME MORE DIFFICULT MOVES

1. Buy a smaller car, less expensive to operate. However, don't make the mistake of buying that smaller car before you need it. Smaller cars, though they may use less gasoline, are expensive. In some cases cars getting more than 20 miles per gallon cost considerably more than even newer cars that yield only 15 miles per gallon.

Calculate the number of miles you drive per year and the gallons of gasoline you will need. Then figure the difference between the value of your present car and a newer, smaller one, which would give better mileage. You might discover that it is far less expensive to continue to drive your old V8 than to buy a one- or two-year-old, four-cylinder, imported or domestic car.

In 1980 I priced a new Toyota, four-cylinder, five-speed automobile, and the list price was over $8000. The dealer would not discount it because, "I can sell all of these cheap-to-operate cars I can get."

The average new-car loan in 1980 cost 12% in Minneapolis. This means the interest on $8000 would be $960 the first year, or $80 per month. At 1980 gasoline prices, this would buy almost 70 gallons of gasoline.

If your present car gets 15 miles per gallon, interest alone on the new car loan would buy enough gas to travel

1050 miles per month. This works out to 12,600 miles per year—just to cover the interest.

Obviously, as the new car gets older and the loan is reduced, the amount of interest will decline, but the amount spent for repairs will probably increase—to a greater extent than on your older car, which may not have as many expensive-to-maintain features.

If it's inexpensive transportation you are looking for, the purchase of a newer and smaller car might not be the answer. Continuing to drive your old full-size automobile could be the cheapest thing you can do.

Besides that, the new car is likely to have higher state license fees and insurance cost, carry a sales tax when you purchase it, and other hidden costs, such as the average $100 to the dealer for something called "dealer preparation," and other "necessities," including undercoating in northern states.

Don't get caught in the "economical new car" trap. It could be the most expensive economy you fall into this year. If your old car really is worn out, and few of them ever reach that stage, shop carefully for a replacement.

In Europe and other parts of the world, people consider a car to be a long-term investment. It is not at all unusual to drive the same automobile 10 to 12 years. When you know you are going to drive it that long, you treat it much more gently. You don't let it sit outside uncovered. Even though a garage might not be available, you can buy a canvas or plastic cover to tie over it.

You wash it more often, particularly if you live in a climate where salt can get on it. You wax it more often, you sweep it out more often, you make sure the tires are properly inflated, and you change the oil frequently.

I once had a friend who said his ego demanded that he have a new car every two years, just like all of his business friends. However, as he discovered it would cost him at least $3000 to trade for a new car, he decided to settle for new paint on the old one. At that time, the painting cost $69.95. When he drove out with a brand-new color, he was just as filled with pride and satisfaction as if the whole car were right off the assembly line.

I frequently hear people say, "My car is just about ready for a new set of tires and a new battery, and I'm sure that the brake linings must be getting thin, so it makes a lot of sense for me to buy a new car." So they take their $1000 car and trade it in on a brand-new $8000 car, and end up with a $7000 mortgage and monthly payments of $204.92 over the next three-and-a-half years.

What would the new tires, battery, and brake linings cost, even if you did need them all? A first-class battery cost about $50 in 1980. By watching for sales you could get a set of four excellent new tires for not more than $150, and the brake linings shouldn't come to more than $150. Total cost: $350, and total investment in the old car: $1350 (1980 prices).

Total investment in a new car: $8000, with monthly payments of $204.92 for 42 months. In just two months of payments on the new car, you would have totally paid off the cost of fixing up the old car.

I have nothing against buying new cars, providing one condition exists. If you can pay for the new car out of your savings, without having to finance it, go ahead and get the new one if you need it. However, if you have to borrow money to buy that new car, it is an unwise move to make. Solomon gave us a word of caution on this: "Borrow money and you are the lender's slave" (Prov. 22:7).

Now, with that said, if you do find yourself in real need of a different car and don't have the cash to buy it, shop around for a car loan. Terms are not the same from bank to bank, finance company to finance company, or credit union to credit union.

When money is tight and interest rates are high, some lenders save their car loan money for regular customers. Consequently, someone walking in off the street finds it difficult to get a loan. But most are looking for good customers.

The chief measure of what a loan costs is the annual percentage rate (APR)—interest that takes into account the shrinking balance of the loan. By federal law, lenders must tell you the APR and put it in writing before signing you up. In any given locality, APRs will vary, often by several percentage points.

In 1980 in the Minneapolis area the APRs for new-car loans ranged from 12% to 17%. By borrowing at the lowest rate, you'd save $561 over the term of a three-year $5800 loan, which is close to the average amount borrowed on new cars today.

As car prices have risen, the length of car loans has increased. The three-year loan was standard as recently as 1977, but 54% of all dealer-financed loans are now for three and a half years and lenders say that the four-year loan is moving up fast. Five-year loans are also available, but they are far from common and are restricted mainly to expensive cars or cars that are known to keep their value unusually well.

If you are forced to take out a loan to purchase a car, there is at least one benefit. You can deduct the interest from your income before calculating your taxes, if you itemize your deductions. A second, somewhat more elusive advantage, is that if inflation will remain high, you'll be paying back the debt in "cheaper" dollars. (See the end of this chapter for sources of auto loans.)

2. Buy a used car. A friend whose take-home pay was $500 per month rolled into the parking lot with a new car that had cost her at least $5000. Her old car was not worth more than $500, so she financed $4500 of it. The cost of

that loan would be approximately $131.74 per month for 42 months at current interest rates, plus insurance of $38.20 per month for a total monthly cost of $169.94. That's what her transportation is costing her before she buys her state license, or puts the first drop of gasoline in the tank—34% of her take-home pay.

By coincidence that same week, another friend purchased a 1966 Corvair which had only 24,000 miles on it. Not only did it look good and run well and got better mileage than the new car my friend bought, but the insurance, the license tax, and every other part of the upkeep was much less.

The Corvair (which is typical of the many excellent older cars available if you look around) cost $1500. If all of that was financed at 12% for a period of 42 months, the payments would be $43.91 per month. The total cost of driving the Corvair, including the insurance, but before state license or gasoline, is $69.72 per month. Had my friend purchased a good used car like this one instead of the new one, that would have been 14% of her take-home pay instead of 34%.

Don't be afraid of driving five- and ten-year-old cars. If the previous owners took care of them, and if you select them with a little thought and guidance by friends who know used cars, you may discover that you have purchased a car that holds its value and may even increase. Buying used cars instead of new ones will always bring an argument, but if you are still in doubt, seek the advice of a knowledgeable friend. Remember Solomon's advice: "Get all the advice you can, and you will succeed; without it you will fail" (Prov. 15:22).

If you buy a used car, shop carefully. The convenience of going to a dealer is that you can look at many offerings at each stop. The dealer will also take care of the financing if you need to borrow money, but I hope you'll buy only what you can pay for in cash.

Don't be reluctant to read the want ads and then to deal with a private party. If you have an established bank account and your record is good, or if you have a small savings account, you will find the bank willing to loan money to buy a car.

The bigger the car you buy, and the more electrical gadgets it has, the greater the chance of failures and expensive repairs. Power windows, power seats, air conditioning, electric trunk unlockers, and radios with tape decks are nice luxuries. However, they all wear out after they've been used a few years. In addition, the bigger cars require bigger tires and batteries.

Forego a little of the luxury and the prestige that goes with an air-conditioned "gunboat," and buy something that will give you dependable transportation, reasonably good mileage, the assurance of fewer things to wear out, and lower costs to repair those that do.

To buy a used car that will give you the lowest cost per mile, look at a two- to four-year-old car by a well-known automaker, with less than 40,000 miles on the odometer. Look for a car that has not been repainted. Repainting is not necessary on a car less than four years old, unless it has been abused either by neglect resulting in body rust and other damage, or through accidents. Check the battery, tires, brake linings, muffler, and work orders covering any other repairs. If none of these things has been replaced, you can count on having to do them. But if they've been done recently, you could be buying a car with two or three years of relatively maintenance-free service left in it.

Insurance costs on used cars will be lower; bias belted tires used on the older cars are less expensive than the radial tires used on the newer ones; annual state license fees are less; and the used car will go just as fast, just as comfortably, and just as dependably as one that will cost two to ten times as much.

A friend once told me that if we were truly seeking to put God first in our lives, then we could expect to find the right car at the right price. "The Lord knows your need," he told me. "He will provide the right car as you are putting him first in your life."

He told me how he and his wife had prayed, "Lord, we expect this car to come to us at the right time and the right price. We thank you for it. Amen." And it did. "If you believe, you will receive whatever you ask for in prayer" (Matt. 21:22).

I hope you will not buy another car, no matter how old it is, unless your present one has collapsed and you can pay cash. Join the people who look at their cars as a lifetime investment. If you do that too, the car will serve you for years.

3. Another way to avoid the high cost of gasoline is to buy a motorcycle. Until recently, cycles were strictly adult toys and teenage transportation. But now more and more business and professional people think it's a way to beat the high cost of getting around.

At first glance, it makes sense. But at second glance, a number of problems appear.

First, motorcycles are dangerous. I have ridden them for more than 25 years, and I've had several narrow escapes. I have observed that most people who drive automobiles act as if they can't see motorcyclists, so you must ride them as though you were absolutely invisible. Make no mistake, motorcycles are dangerous vehicles, regardless of the number of years experience you might have in riding them.

Second, the cost of motorcycles now frequently exceeds the cost of a compact automobile. It's not uncommon to pay from $2000 to $3000 or more for a good motorcycle. That's a large investment just to save money on gasoline. Paying $3000 for a motorcycle, and leaving your car in the garage, means that you've just laid out enough money to buy 2500 gallons of gasoline at 1980 prices. If your car gets 15 miles to the gallon, you've spent enough money to drive your car 37,500 miles, and for an average driver that's at least three to four years of driving.

The cost of buying the motorcycle, as with the car, is only the beginning. You also have the annual license fee and the insurance, which is not cheap because of the number of accidents people have with motorcycles.

Regardless of where you live, if your job requires a reasonable appearance, and perhaps even a suit and necktie, you're in for some problems. The sun might be shining on the way to work, but the weather could turn rainy before you leave for home. That nicely pressed suit and neat necktie could need a trip to the cleaners at the end of the day.

In colder climates it's not only the occasional rain you must gamble with, but in the wintertime, the ice, snow, and cold force the motorcycle into storage. Now your $3000 investment is also costing you money for storage as well as those monthly payments or lost interest income if you'd left your money in the bank. In warmer climates if you have to appear at work in a fresh and clean condition, you might find yourself arriving hot, dirty, and sweaty.

In Chapter 1 we noted the financial problems of John and Mary, who, among other things, had purchased a motorcycle to reduce their transportation costs. All it did was drive them closer to bankruptcy and risk the safety and health of the young breadwinner. One of the first things I asked them to do was sell their motorcycle. A little of his *macho* went with it, but the young wife was relieved when the cycle went out the door.

Sure they're fun to ride, and they're fun to have. But it's still not reliable transportation. It is strictly a luxury and an unnecessary toy.

4. A mini-motorcycle, or a motorized bicycle, called a moped, is another option. For years these have been popular in Europe, but in America, mopeds make little sense as basic transportation, particularly if they are an attempt to reduce transportation costs.

You still have insurance and license fees; you still get wet when it rains; you still can't carry much; you must have a place to tuck it away in inclement weather; you still have to worry about thieves; you still have to drive as though you were invisible; you still risk serious injury from collisions with automobiles; and you still have to own an automobile if you have a family, want someone to travel with you, want to carry anything, or live in a part of the country that has winter as well as summer.

Mopeds, like motorcycles, are recreational vehicles. It is not a useful alternative method of transportation which will reduce your cost of transportation in a time of inflation. It will merely add one more piece of mechanical equipment to maintain, insure, operate, and store.

5. Lease a car. Under certain circumstances it might be to your advantage to lease a car, but you have to remember that the leasing company must cover their expenses and make a profit as well. Leasing a new car costs about 40% more than buying one for cash.

The advantage of leasing is that you can get a new, or nearly new, car with no money down, and with monthly payments that are usually smaller than loan payments. But because you have no equity in the car at the end of the lease, it is more expensive to lease than to buy.

For example, if you took out a typical two-year lease on

a new $5500 Dodge Aspen, the monthly fee would be about $190, including state tax. Two years' use of the car would cost you $4560. If you made a 20% down payment ($1000) and took out a two-year loan for $4400 at 13% to buy the same car, the monthly payments would be $209. At the loan's end you would have paid $6116 ($1000 down plus $5016 in payments), or $1556 more than if you had leased it, and you would have tied up the down payment of $1200 for two years, instead of earning approximately $200 interest on it. So the total cost of purchasing the car would be $6116 + $200 = $6316. If your car was then worth $3222 (typical 1979 Blue Book figure for a two-year-old Aspen), your net cost to purchase would have been $3094, or $1466 less than leasing.

An increasingly popular leasing alternative is to lease used cars, or what is called secondary leasing. The automobile rental companies lease new cars for one or two years and sometimes longer. When these are turned back, the leasing company has the option of selling them or re-leasing them. It's when they are re-leased that you can get good cars at lower prices and bring your cost for transportation below what it would be if you financed the purchase of a new car. If you're going to check out leasing, check out the leasing of secondhand cars, and go with the reputable leasing companies to minimize the risk of poor maintenance or poor service.

6. For some, the best answer may be public transportation. Many cities have buses, subways, electric aboveground trolleys, and even fancier public transportation, such as a monorail. But in most cities they have been neglected by the public. We have preferred the freedom of having our own automobile at our disposal 24 hours a day.

Public transportation is now coming into its own. People are discovering the joys of getting on a bus nearby, being able to read a newspaper while someone is driving them downtown, and getting off just a block from their offices without having to pay a $2.50 daily parking fee.

The bus or train ticket is less than the cost of gasoline alone, not even counting the cost of insurance, license fees, depreciation, parking, and maintenance.

If your car gets 20 miles to the gallon, and you drive 20 miles to work, pay $3 a day to park, and then drive 20 miles back home again, the total cost just for gasoline and parking is more than $5 per day. If you add insurance, depreciation, repairs, and license fee, you've probably paid closer to $7 per day to drive that car to work. If public transportation costs you a dollar each way, you will be saving $5 each day.

SOURCES OF AUTO LOANS

Where do you go for a loan to buy your automobile? Here are four suggestions:

Credit unions. This will probably be your first choice if you belong to one, for here you would fare better than anywhere else. The average cost for a car loan in most areas in 1980 was 10.8% to 12%.

Banks are the best second choice. Try your own bank first. Bank interest rates in 1980 were in the 11% to 12.5% range.

Automobile dealers are the third choice. It's easier for you to buy the car and obtain the loan at one place. However, the interest rate is generally higher, ranging from approximately 11.5% to as high as 17.5% in at least one West Coast area in 1980. Also in 1980 the Federal Reserve reported the average commercial bank's APR was 11.6%, compared with 13.3% APR for dealers.

Finance companies should be considered only as a last resort. In a number of states in 1980 you could not get enough money from them to finance an expensive car since the legal limit on the size of finance company loans was low—$2000 in New York, for instance. In states where the limit is higher, you're likely to be charged the maximum interest rate the law allows. For example, the maximum interest on a three-year loan of $5000 in Idaho was 20.5% in 1980.

So, where does this leave you as you try to fight inflating costs of transportation?

More three-car families will become two-car families, and more two-car families will become one-car families. Many who bought a new car every two years will find that the old one will not accumulate quite as many miles every year and will easily last four or five years or more. They'll experience the thrill of making the final mortgage payment on the last car they purchased and discover that the money previously committed to those monthly payments can now go into savings or investments. Since automobiles are the second or third highest cost for most people, reducing the number of cars will open a whole new way of life. And more people in our country will do without cars.

Finally, it's worth repeating the biblical admonitions to "be satisfied with what we have," "live within our income," and "stay out of debt." We can do all three and still have reliable transportation.

5

More for
Your Food Dollar

*Why spend money on what does
not satisfy? Why spend your
wages and still be hungry? (Isa.
55:2)*

Isaiah was speaking principally of spiritual food in this
passage, but the analogy is to real food, food that did not
satisfy — perhaps "junk food," cigarettes, alcohol, and
other things unnecessary and even damaging to health. If
we really want to cut the amount of money we are spending at grocery stores, a good place to start is with these
foods that do not satisfy. Another place is to cut down on
waste. In America about 10% of all food purchased is
thrown in the garbage. Much food rots before it is eaten
because of poor buying or poor meal planning. Some of
it is thrown out because too much is prepared for one
meal; some is thrown out because we are too lazy to store
leftovers in our refrigerators and make that special effort
to prepare meals from them.

An interesting thing is happening as Americans struggle
to stay abreast of the rising costs of everything in our inflationary economy. Although we are spending a higher percentage of our income on housing, utilities, and health,

we are finding ways to spend less and less of our income, percentagewise, on food and drink. According to U.S. Department of Commerce figures, in 1950 we spent 28.06% of our income on food. By 1960, it had dropped to 24.86%, by 1972 to 20.30%, and by 1978 to 19.91 cents out of every dollar.

Shoppers know that it is seldom less expensive to buy fresh vegetables even when they are in season than it is to buy canned vegetables. They also know that grocery stores frequently run "loss leaders," which are real bargains. The grocers hope that these "loss leaders" will get you into the store, where you will buy more things which might even be higher than at competitive stores.

American food buyers also know how to take advantage of weekly specials and discount coupons, and they're not usually fooled by phony bargains.

But an even more fundamental change seems to be taking place in American food buying and eating habits. We simply avoid eating food we think is priced too high. When the price of beef rose sharply in the mid 1970s, the per capita consumption dropped off considerably. Americans turned to poultry, fish, and a heavier reliance on vegetables.

At another extreme, there seems to be a trend among at least some people to discontinue eating meat altogether. Some claim to do it because it is more healthful and, if it works, that's reason enough. Still others have done so because of the high price of meat, and that is an equally valid reason.

Then when the price of fruit and fresh vegetables climbed sharply because of strikes, the food shoppers turned to canned goods, dairy products, wheat products, or home-grown produce. In past years, when inflationary pressures had not moved other prices so high, consumers would have been much more likely to simply pay the higher prices rather than change their diets.

American food buyers refuse to stand still and be taken advantage of during a period when prices are rising so rapidly. They avoid buying the most expensive items and are not reluctant to change eating patterns to hold down the price of food.

TIPS ON FOOD BUYING

1. The best way to avoid buying too much is to prepare a shopping list before going to the supermarket. Prepare a week's menus in advance, and do not, except under unusual circumstances, buy anything not on your grocery list.

Grocers know that most of us are "impulse buyers." This means that if we see a grocery cart full of canned peas in the middle of the aisle, with a big SPECIAL card on it, we are likely to add three or six cans to our shopping baskets, even if we don't need peas.

Likewise, when we are in the middle of a "meatless week," but see a big sign on the meat counter, SPECIAL ON GROUND BEEF, we are likely to add a few pounds to our basket.

Even though it is recommended that you stay within your shopping list for the week, on rare occasions some staple food may be on sale. If it is food you use on a regular basis and you know it will be on your list in a week or two, it may be all right to buy it. But make sure it's something you use often and not unneeded luxury food.

If you find that your definition of *staple* expands a little when you see things on sale, go back to the basic rule of buying only what's on your list, bargain or no bargain.

2. Food coupons and cash refunds are inducements to get shoppers into a store, and are popular sales tech-

niques. The coupons give you discounts on the prices of certain foods and are usually very attractive.

Grocery coupons are worth an average of 15¢ each, while the average refund offer has a $1.25 value. Even though this amount may seem small, those who use coupons carefully, trade the ones they can't use with friends, keep every offer they find, watch for "double discounts," and make a real study out of it, claim they can trim food expenses by 25%, and some even claim by 50%.

Later we will hear from a coupon shopper, but as she uses coupon terminology in her explanation, we need some definitions first.

Cash-offs. The term "cash-off coupons," or just "cash-offs," refers to those coupons in the newspapers which say that if you buy a half-gallon of bleach and present that particular coupon, the grocer will give you a discount. You are getting some "cash off."

Some "cash-offs" have a limited time period during which they can be used, and others have no time limit. The ones with no limit are usually saved by prudent shoppers until the grocery store runs a special on the product. When you subtract the "cash-off" from the sale price, it becomes a real bargain. Manufacturers offered about 81 billion cents-off coupons in 1979. Only 4.2% of those were redeemed, even though 80% of American households use coupons.

Refund form. Refund forms are usually found on pads in almost every grocery store, often near the checkout counter or below the product advertised. You must fill out these forms, then mail them to the manufacturer of the product you have purchased with some POP (proof of purchase), which is usually found on the package. When the manufacturer receives the refund form with the POP, he will send you a check or cash.

Refund checks run from minor amounts, such as 35-50¢

up to several dollars, or coupons for free products. An experienced refund shopper, however, will not bother using postage for anything less than a dollar refund.

In most cases, refund offers are limited to one per family or address and carry an expiration date by which all refund forms with proofs of purchase must be received. There are exceptions, however, in the number of offers available for participation, and quite a few offers with no expiration date.

Most refund offers require the purchase of one or more of the same product and sending in the required proof of purchase. Some are on anywhere from two to five products, and your refund will be based on the number of products you purchase and proofs sent in. About 7000 refund offers were made in 1979, according to *The Supermarket Shoppers 1980 Guide to Coupons and Refunds.*

Refunding. A few of the larger food and household supply manufacturers provide little booklets into which you can paste the coupons or POP found on their products at various times.

For example, you will find a proof of purchase triangle on a roll of paper toweling. By cutting off those triangles and pasting them into the book, eventually you will fill the book and mail it back to the manufacturer with a request for the cash refund.

These cash refunds come to you either by check or certificate good for the purchase of an amount of that company's product equal to the value of the refund booklet. These frequently are in the $1 to $7 category, and are tax-free income.

The business of reducing food costs by using various kinds of cash-offs, manufacturers' refunds, and cash refunds, when combined with watching for sales or specials, can result in the examples below.

Here is what one careful shopper reported:

"I once watched a TV show about 'Refundable Bundles.' I was already seeking ways to find the forms which are required on about 75% of the food refunds. I wrote to the show, asked for more information and received a listing of newsletters put out by enterprising housewives around the country. I subscribed to one published by a woman known as the Coupon Queen. The TV show had filmed her shopping for groceries, and she had purchased $107 worth of groceries and paid a total of $6. The rest was covered in cash-offs and free-food forms (coupons that give a cash-off discount from your total food purchase) obtained through her refund activities."

Refunding is available on food, cleaning supplies, paper products, cosmetics, drugs, hair products, appliances, and some sports equipment. The key is to obtain the forms. Some areas of the country are not particularly good about putting them out. However, the newsletters do have a section for refunders (people who use coupons regularly) to advertise form exchanges; or by sending a small fee or stamps, they will send you a selection of forms. Trading is usually one for one. Or, they will ask for current "qualifiers," and will offer 5 to 10 forms per qualifier you send them. "Qualifiers" are those proofs of purchase the manufacturer may require, and these are evenly exchanged as well.

Manufacturers may some day move to refunding exclusively because of the many fraudulent activities on the part of some to reproduce cash-offs illegally. Refunds run from 50¢ to $5, $7, and even $10.

Seeking product loyalty, manufacturers are putting more and more of their advertising and public relations money into this scheme of saving. In Eastern states, such as New Jersey, New York, and Pennsylvania, grocery stores have one day during the week in which they match every cash-off customers bring in. With regular cash-offs, refund cash-offs, or free-food forms it becomes worthwhile to shop at such stores.

Paper towels, tissues, and toilet tissue are some examples. All have doubled in price in the decade of the 1970s, and all are used in sales. Here is an example of why it saves to buy in quantity on items that we use constantly. Our shopping reporter continued:

"In 1979 a local store ran an ad on all three of the above products, and all were national brands. Paper towels selling for 99¢ were reduced to 69¢ on a special. By the case they came to 49¢ a roll. Taking my already saved up cash-offs to the store reduced my price to 39¢ a roll. I saved the proofs of purchase since I had read about a paper towel offer good in the Eastern states and had determined by reading the newsletter that the offer would eventually come to Minneapolis. When it did, for 24 proofs of purchase I received a $7 coupon good at any grocery store. My original purchase of 24 rolls cost $9.36 on sale and with cash-offs. With an additional $7 off now on my groceries, my paper towels came to $2.36 or less than 10¢ a roll, an overall saving of 90%.

"At the same sale I bought Kleenex in the same quantity. It is priced from 71¢ to 83¢ per box in most stores, but at the discount store it was being sold for 49¢ a box. With my already saved cash-offs, it averaged out to 37¢ a box. Kleenex had an offer out at that time for a $3 refund for 10 proofs of purchase. Since I had bought some Kleenex for my daughter, I sent in two refund forms. I spent $8.88 for 24 boxes of Kleenex and received a cash refund of $6. This made the cost of the Kleenex 12¢ a box."

Here are some other examples: "A 9-ounce tube of Colgate toothpaste regularly retails for $1.39 to $1.49. I bought 10 tubes on sale for 89¢ each; my cash-offs of 25¢ per tube made my price 64¢ a tube, for a total expenditure of $6.40. I sent in two refund offers of $2 each for three proofs of purchase ($4). My total expenditure was $2.40 for 10 tubes, or 24¢ each. The same was held true on laundry detergent, fabric softener, and dish washer detergent."

Here are some rules:

- Never buy without the cash-offs and never buy unless the above products are on sale.
- Never shop without carrying coupons and cash-offs in the event you run into sales of products you *know* will be used.
- Never buy a product you would not normally use just to take advantage of a refund offer or big cash-off.
- Be willing to switch national brands for good prices or good offers. Quality control dictates that national brands will be similar in quality.

The Board of Editors of the various refund newsletters took a survey recently which showed the average refund family to be two adults and one pet (larger families would have far greater savings), who spent $120-150 a year on postage and envelopes and averaged $300 a year in *cash* refunds. That does not include the free-food coupons refunded, nor the cash-offs clipped from papers and magazines. Grocery store ads often run their own coupons. If the item is one you want to buy anyway, you use their coupon, plus the cash-off the manufacturer has offered. Both are good on the same item.

"I deposit about $20 a month on cash refunds. Regular cash-offs will take 7-10% off the grocery bill. Free-food coupons really do the job. One day I stopped at a supermarket to buy a few items. I bought $18 worth of groceries and paid 3¢ at the checkout counter! Another day my bill came to a little over $17, and I came out exactly even. These incidents portray the extreme, but these savings do help."

Obviously, we cannot buy all the products necessary to participate in all refunds. So we trade the appropriate qualifiers. Most people will not take the time necessary to become involved. It helps to have a goal.

If you can use the coupons at the store where you normally shop, or one within a few blocks of your home, if they are for basic foods or food you normally buy, and if you can restrict your buying of other things while you are there, they are a game well worth playing. However, if you have to drive great distances from store to store in order to take advantage of the coupons, you'll probably end up paying more for gasoline than you'll save from the reduced cost of food.

Coupons can be a way to save money on the purchase of food, but only if you recognize the other costs that go into using them.

News articles about the success of refunding may be found regularly in magazines such as *Family Circle, Today's Woman,* and *Reader's Digest.*

"The Today Show," "Good Morning America," and many other daytime talk shows are now featuring one of the many "Coupon Queens," most of whom are also publishers of one of the many bulletins now available. Annual subscription rates on these monthly bulletins run anywhere from $7 to $12 per year. In early 1980 there were approximately 70 such publications available.

3. Never go shopping when you are hungry. If you do you are much more susceptible to impulse buying, and you'll go over your food budget to get that rotisserie chicken or those fresh bakery rolls.

A friend of ours began spending 25% more on groceries and couldn't figure out why. Then it occurred to her that ever since she had begun fasting on her shopping day, her hunger had caused her to purchase more than ever before.

4. What about farmers' markets? Although farmers know the pricing of retail stores and have raised their own prices accordingly, there are nearly 800 farmers' markets nationally where city dwellers can buy direct from the producer, an increase of nearly 60% in the late 1970s. The food at such markets includes vegetables, fruits, sausages, country hams. They are often cheaper than similar foods in supermarkets.

5. Go and pick your own. Increasingly, farmers faced with their own high labor-costs are opening up their fields to consumers willing to pick their own vegetables and fruits. By picking it yourself you can buy a quart of berries in one area, for example, for approximately 70¢, compared to $1 or more in the supermarket. But you must consider the cost of getting there.

6. Buy surplus and day-old bread. Hundreds of the nation's large bakeries operate retail outlets where surplus and day-old bread and other items are sold. Prices are often 25% or more below retail, and you can store what you buy in your freezer.

7. Does it pay to buy meat in quantities? Meat in quantity can be purchased from supermarkets, meat processors, and even directly from farmers. These savings are usually slim because most supermarkets already reduce meat prices hoping to make their profits on other items in the store. In addition, beef carcasses are sold by weight before cutting or trimming, and up to 30% of that weight could be lost in the process. You must also be wary of "bait and switch" ads, the kind that promise good deals but when you get there you find they are out of those good deals (the bait), and they sell you something else much more expensive (the switch).

8. How about group purchasing? Some people are using other ways to take advantage of wholesale buying to save 10% to 40% on food prices. Several neighbors or

friends band together and buy cases of canned goods from wholesalers, or several sides of beef from meat processors. Then they cooperatively rent space in a frozen food locker and, with good sharp bookkeeping, come out ahead. Going together to buy 100 cases of canned goods from a wholesaler is an excellent way to cut your food costs. But, of course, you will need the cash to do it.

9. Take advantage of weekly specials. If you live in an area near several supermarkets, be sure to check the ads to take advantage of specials. You can usually plan your menus around these specials. But don't drive to a distant store to pick up a bargain when the extra fuel will nullify any saving.

10. Cook two meals at one time. Many meal planners frequently cook double the amount needed for one meal, packaging the excess and freezing it for another meal.

11. Buy fresh fruits and vegetables only when they are in season.

12. Figure the cost of fruit, sugar, and canning supplies and decide how much savings there is before canning or freezing anything.

13. Use nonfat dry milk for cooking. For family use, if you have the time, mix it with whole milk to make it taste better.

14. Compare appearance with price. For example, are canned whole beets worth more than the same amount of diced beets that are less expensive? Are the redder, more expensive apples better than the not-so-red apples?

15. Use medium instead of sharp cheese. Purchase house brands instead of national brands when they cost less, which is almost always.

16. Give children snacks with food value, such as granola, nuts, cheese, fruit, and cottage cheese instead of nonnutritive potato chips, candy, or pop. Sometimes

nutritious foods cost more, but when health factors are compared, the value is always on the side of nutrition.

17. Purchase meat on the basis of cost per serving instead of cost per pound. Buy roasts instead of steaks. Learn to substitute soy beans in the form of texturized vegetable protein for hamburger. Extreme care should be used when beef is bought in bulk. Waste and poor quality often make a seemingly good buy a bad one. Usually meat bought during a sale at the supermarket is a better buy than meat bought in bulk.

18. Stay away from prepared foods, or allow only one night a week for pizza and similar items. These cost much more than they are worth in food value.

19. If possible, shop without the pressure of having your children with you.

20. TV dinners are usually well-balanced nutritionally and, when on special, are an inexpensive way to eat.

21. Buy staples such as flour and sugar, and bake your own cakes instead of using expensive mixes.

22. Buy store label (generic) products. They often sell for 30% to 60% less than name brands, and can cut your total grocery bill by 15% to 20%, according to Gary Dickson, founder of the "FM Refunders Club."

23. Eat less. Most of us eat far more than we need. We'll feel better and be more healthy if we do.

DIFFERENT KINDS OF STORES

It also may save you money if you check the various types of food stores in your area. The difference in prices will vary and depends on many things. Here are some alternatives:

1. **Co-ops.** If you have more time than money, a co-op food store might be the answer. It is necessary to scoop

dry staples from their bulk containers and weigh them yourself, but in doing so you can buy only as much as you need. If you don't have 59¢ for a two-pound bag of flour at a regular store, you can buy just two cups for about 10¢ at a co-op. Co-ops excel in spice and herb values.

Co-ops are barely competitive, and sometimes more expensive, when it comes to packaged goods such as frozen orange juice. However, if you can only make one trip to a store, it might still be worthwhile to buy these at a co-op.

Volunteer labor keeps food co-ops going, and the extra money you might pay for packaged goods can be eliminated if you can volunteer for a few hours a month: four hours' time will earn up to a 20% discount in some co-ops. Senior citizens get at least a 10% discount at most co-ops.

2. **No-frills stores.** Another low-cost type of store that requires more shopping time is a "no-frills" store. Here the produce must be put in containers by the shopper, and at the checkout counter the shopper bags the groceries and carries them out. A strong back helps, and a car is almost a necessity when shopping at these stores. Many are on bus lines, but if you're going to a no-frills store to stock up on cheap staples, you might not be able to carry the bags home yourself.

The no-frills store can be a problem for people on a limited weekly income because they don't always carry the smallest, cheapest jars and cans. But you can cut food costs 25 to 40% at "no-frills" stores, according to *U.S. News & World Report,* July 7, 1980).

3. **Regular stores.** Regular grocery stores might be most practical on a low budget if you have a little more money than time. All goods are prepackaged, and checkout is

handled by a competent staff, which saves time for the shopper, but it means the stores can't offer the discounted prices of no-frills or co-op stores, except on the weekly or daily specials. But the convenience and better selection might make this best for you.

EATING OUT

Some restaurant people predict that by the middle 1980s the average American family will be eating 50% of its meals in restaurants. That we are already approaching that figure is evidenced by the tremendous number of fast-food franchises.

Some people say it's cheaper to eat out than at home, and in some instances that may be true. For example, if you live by yourself and have a hard time finding a grocery store where you can buy single portions, your leftovers that might be wasted could be enough to offset the higher cost of restaurant food.

However, the restaurant has to pay employees to buy the food, cook it, serve it, clean up the kitchen, and wash the dishes. It also has to pay rent on the building it occupies and the equipment it leases or purchases. On top of these expenses, it must make a profit. There's no way it can pay all these people and the other overhead costs, make a profit, and still feed you less expensively than you can eat at home, if you follow reasonably prudent food purchasing and handling practices of your own. If you don't buy the most expensive foods and don't throw away much in waste, eating at home is less expensive.

Watch for the specials when you eat out, as you do at the food stores. Make eating out a treat, rather than misleading yourself into thinking the reason is to save money. For families and for most people, it's a nice outing, but it is simply not less expensive.

Why not have a "food brainstorming party" with a few friends? Have each submit one idea, in writing, on some way to save money on food. Read and discuss the ideas. Everyone will go home richer for the experience.

6

Saving Money on Furniture and Clothes

Keep your lives free from the love of money, and be satisfied with what you have. For God has said, "I will never leave you; I will never abandon you" (Heb. 13:5).

Steady inflation has raised the question of whether you are ahead by borrowing money to buy things before the price goes up, or saving until you can buy for cash.

Some think it's much better to borrow if necessary to buy now. This is not very sound advice. Most things bought "before the price goes up" aren't really needed, and you should consider the unnecessary problems if something does go wrong.

BUYING FURNITURE

Consider Betty and Bob, a well-off young couple who want to buy a $300 stereo. If they save $25 a month, they will have the $300 at the end of the year. At a 5¼% passbook savings rate, compounded quarterly, they will have earned about $8.50 in interest.

If Betty and Bob are in the 36% federal tax bracket,

higher than most, they will owe about $3 in federal taxes on the interest earned on the savings account, leaving net income on savings of about $5.50.

In the meantime, the price of the stereo, assuming inflation continues, will have risen to about $327, 9% more than a year ago. The couple will have lost a net of $21.50 by waiting to save for the stereo, and they will have "wasted" the year listening to a tiny transistor.

But what if the couple instead got a $300 cash advance on a VISA or Mastercharge card and bought the stereo right away? In some states they would be paying 12% interest on the advance (although in many states it's 18% annually). Minimum monthly repayment would be about $26.50, and the total interest cost at year's end when the debt is paid off would total $18.

Since interest payments can be deducted in determining taxable income, the real after-tax interest payments will be less than $12—the $18 reduced by their 36% tax saving. Betty and Bob would have avoided the $27 price increase on the stereo by buying it now. By subtracting the $12 after-tax interest they paid, they would have saved $15 and they would have use of the stereo for the whole 12 months. Is that the whole story?

To save $15 they would have run themselves $300 into debt for something they probably didn't need in the first place. Such savings are insignificant compared to the loss of peace of mind that inevitably results from installment debt. Installment purchase might also have resulted in the loss of the stereo set plus all they had paid down on it, if either Bob or Betty had lost their jobs.

It may be wise to borrow money at times during inflation, but if the price you have to pay is anxiety, tension, and possible loss of everything if your income is reduced or cut off, trying to ride that inflation bucking bronco is too much of a risk.

John and Mary, the young couple described in Chapter 1, who bought two full rooms of furniture for "only" $875, made two mistakes. First, they paid the full retail price of new furniture, and second, they got cheaply constructed furniture.

Sometimes it is best to buy something new. A personal item such as a mattress or complete bed would be such a case for many people. But if they are already short of cash and loaded with installment payments, the better choice is to buy used furniture or none.

What Mary and John could have done was pick up secondhand furniture for little or nothing. If either of their parents, or older brothers or sisters, uncles, aunts, or grandparents had been asked, they could probably have furnished a one-bedroom apartment. Almost everyone who has had an established home for any length of time has extra pieces of furniture.

A second preferable source of furniture is secondhand stores. The Salvation Army, Goodwill Industries, and similar organizations accumulate donated furniture. At one time only those who could not afford new furniture shopped at secondhand furniture stores. Now you'll find those well able to buy any kind of furniture for cash looking for prize older pieces because they look "quaint," have "character," or might actually be choice antiques.

A third place is the want ads in your daily newspaper. Some may be junk, some almost new, but all are cheaper than the new prices in a retail store.

Garage and moving sales are particularly popular places for such shopping and have become regular weekly events for bargain shoppers.

Usually overlooked is the want-ad column that advertises business equipment for sale. Occasionally businesses will refurnish or close out older locations and move to new offices, or even go out of business altogether. Every office seems to have at least some furniture that is appropriate for a home. The manager's office may have a couch and one or two comfortable chairs, a coffee table, table lamps, maybe even the draperies. Others will have conference tables suitable for dining room tables, and chairs to match.

Furniture from business offices has probably been fully depreciated on the company books. Even if not depreciated and sold for less than "book value," the "loss" can be taken as a business expense. Consequently, the business remodeling its office, replacing its furniture, moving, or going out of business, is likely to have a roomful of bargains. Even though the ad starts out with addressing equipment, electric typewriters, and electronic calculators, read on. It may say "and many other miscellaneous items of office furniture."

I once responded to such an ad and bought a magnificent solid mahogany conference table and eight comfortable leather chairs for 20% of what they would have cost new. They were less than one year old. Twenty years later, I still have every piece, and all look as good as new.

Had I purchased new equipment, I would have had to get a much lower quality mahogany veneer or, more than likely, some kind of imitation wood table and a much lower quality set of chairs. But I got the best for far less, by being willing to shop and take something not quite new.

When you shop for used furniture, try to answer want ads from people living in the economically more affluent areas of town, or the more affluent suburbs. They are more likely to have purchased high quality furniture, so you are likely to buy a much higher quality of used furniture.

There is a disadvantage to shopping in the second-hand furniture market. Normally, you have to pay cash.

If you buy from a credit furniture store, a department store, or elsewhere, you will normally either be able to finance the purchase or pay on some kind of extended purchase plan.

But coming up with the cash is much the better way to buy and may not be difficult if you have carefully budgeted your expenditures for furniture and all other acquisitions. By planning ahead and by spacing out your furniture purchases, buying first those things that are most needed, you will have the modest amount of cash readily available for each purchase.

Biggest bargains on the used furniture market are television sets. Those brand-new $700 and $800 color television sets can be bought secondhand for $100 to $200. You're taking a chance on the picture tube going out, but even if it does, the entire cost of a new picture tube is not likely to exceed $250 including labor.

In all of the sets built in relatively recent years, the old auxiliary small tubes have been replaced by what is called "solid state" circuits. This means there is very little chance of much else going out except for the picture tube. So your risk is substantially reduced. You know that you can replace the most expensive part of the set a day after you buy it, if you have to, and still come out at about half of what it would cost to buy a new one.

BUYING CLOTHES

Although there is continuous pressure on Americans to buy new clothes and keep up with the styles, more and more Americans feel less compulsion to do so. It's not that they wouldn't like to, but with the cost of everything else going up, they would rather spend any extra money on house payments than on clothes that will hang in the closet 25 days or more each month.

Consequently, men shy away from extreme styles. The extra-wide or narrow lapels are the first to become obsolete, while the middle-size width, as with neckties and collars, seem to be acceptable regardless of the swings in styles.

The same holds true, although to a lesser extent, for women's apparel. Certain types of dresses seem to look nice year after year. Buying basic things applies to women's clothing too. Then each season you can take inventory and match up a blazer with a pair of slacks, or skirt, and blouses or sweaters. By not following the style in length, you will not be outdating your wardrobe when styles move from mini-skirts to skirts way below the calf.

My wife has a floor-length dress which she purchased for the Christmas season some years ago. It is still like new, and she still wears it several times every winter.

Over a period of two years, I bought two pairs of black dress shoes and two pairs of brown ones. They were good quality shoes, and I decided to take care of them to see how long they would last. After eight years they are still in good condition. I keep them polished and make sure that I wear rubbers or overshoes on them in the wintertime so the leather soles do not get wet. I never wear the same pair of shoes two days in a row. The experts tell us shoes need one day to dry out between wearings if they are going to retain their shape and support and continue to be comfortable.

Like most other Americans, I have a pair of tennis shoes, hiking boots, sandals, and thongs. I don't wear them often, and with the exception of the tennis shoes they will probably last as long as I live. I like the jingle, "Use it up, wear it out, make it do, or do without."

So why should I go out and buy a new pair of shoes? More and more people have reached the same conclusion. They would rather buy a good pair of shoes once every three years than buy two or three pairs of cheap shoes every year. Although it's more difficult for women to follow this philosophy than for men, I've noticed that my wife does much the same thing. The bitterness of low quality is remembered long after the sweetness of low price is forgotten.

Clothing is another of those costs of living on which we Americans are spending a declining percentage of our income. In 1950 $11.66 out of every $100 went for clothing; in 1960 the figure had declined to $9.29 per 100, and by 1978 it had come down to $7.20. This means that during that last 18-year period Americans have cut the percentage of their income spent on clothing by 33%.

The average person can still buy stylish clothing and stay current by knowing where the outlets are. Used-clothing stores have sprung up throughout the country. These are not for old discards or rags, but are for dresses, suits, sweaters, and coats that may have been worn only a few times. Perhaps the previous owner put on or lost 20 to 30 pounds, and the clothing no longer fits. Perhaps he or she was financially able to replenish his wardrobe more often and simply got tired of the "old" clothes. You can often buy a well-known brand, even carrying a designer label, for a third or fourth of what it would cost new.

Not only can you find good clothes in used-clothing stores, but they can also be found in garage sales and home sales. Watch the newspapers, and don't be embarrassed by buying someone else's secondhand clothing. They're not embarrassed at putting it up for sale, and if it fits, you've made yourself a good deal.

You might also decide to play this game from the other end. Perhaps you have clothing that you no longer wear but that is in excellent condition. Why not take it to one of those used clothing stores that handle clothing on consignment. If they sell it, they make a commission and you get a few dollars back. If they don't, it generally is given to the Salvation Army or Goodwill, and you may have an income-tax deduction for your contribution.

But the best way to fight the inflationary cost of clothing is simply not to buy as much as you did before. When good friends of ours moved from a large home into a smaller one, they purposely built fewer closets and installed fewer bureau drawers. They forced themselves to dispose of more than half of all the clothing they owned. On moving day they brought along only what they knew they would wear frequently. Everything else stayed behind and was sold.

Their policy now is that they do not buy a single new article of clothing without selling at least one comparable article. Since they hesitate to part with their favorite suits, dresses, shoes, blue jeans, and jackets, they seldom buy anything new. The old has to be "used up and worn out" before anything new comes in their door.

Jesus called us to trust him for our clothing needs. In the Sermon on the Mount, he said:

> Why worry about clothes? Look how the wild flowers grow: they do not work or make clothes for themselves. But I tell you that not even King Solomon with all his wealth had clothes as beautiful as one of these flowers. It is God who clothes the wild grass—grass that is here today and gone tomorrow, burned up in the oven. Won't he be all the more sure to clothe you? What little faith you have!
>
> So do not start worrying: "Where will my food come from? or my drink? or my clothes?" (These are the things the pagans

are always concerned about.) Your Father
in heaven knows that you need all these
things. Instead, be concerned above everything else with the Kingdom of God and with
what he requires of you, and he will provide
you with all these other things. So do not
worry about tomorrow; it will have enough
worries of its own. There is no need to add
to the troubles each day brings (Matt. 6:28-
33).

PRACTICAL TIPS ON CLOTHES

Here are some tips on clothing buying and care that
may sound minor, but a committee of experts say every
one is important.

1. Using too much detergent in your washing machine
can cause stains to appear on some clothing. This is because the rinse cycle in most washing machines cannot
remove all of the detergent if too much has been used.

2. Alternating what you wear from day to day, if you
hang up the clothing not being worn, helps the wrinkles
to smooth out between wearings. This makes them look
better and last longer.

3. Wear the right clothes for the right occasion and
you will also be saving money. Don't do yard work in
a good pair of knit slacks. One snag on a rose bush will
make them inappropriate for dress-up occasions from
that point on. On the other hand, blue jeans are almost
indestructible, roses or no roses.

And, as every cook can tell you, don't wear a good outfit while you are preparing dinner, unless you wear a
cover-up apron. One little splash could ruin it. And always remove any spot you may get on your clothing as
soon as possible. Never leave the spot unattended and

then wash the article in the regular manner. This could set the spot permanently, especially in the newer fabrics (polyester, acrylic) so popular these days.

4. Shopping at thrift stores is a good idea if you know quality, designers, and know how to sew. Much of their merchandise can be made over into very "chic" looking items or may even be designer clothes. It is also possible to purchase from Salvation Army and Goodwill brand-new items that have been contributed by local stores.

5. Shop the insurance company retail outlets. Whenever there is a fire loss in a clothing store, the insurance company normally buys the entire stock by paying off on the insurance. This stock is then resold to a cut-rate insurance liquidation outlet, and there are some excellent buys available. In many cases the clothing is not even damaged by smoke or water, but is simply included because it is much easier to clean out the whole stock than to pick and choose among the garments that might have been damaged.

6. It is far better to buy one good outfit a year than several mediocre items. It is also better to wear the same good-looking outfit over and over than to have several outfits that you never quite feel right in.

Be sure to check the discount stores (K-Mart, Target) when purchasing clothing. If you are a careful shopper, you may be surprised at the attractive outfits you can put together. Often you can find identical styles you would find in the more expensive stores. They may be constructed from less expensive materials, but many times only experts can tell the difference. National chains like Sears, Penney's, and Montgomery Ward are also fine places to shop for quality clothing. Use their mail-order catalogs for additional savings.

7. Sewing your own clothing could be a money saver, but only if you don't sew more than you need, and if you

wear what you sew. There are many home seamstresses whose bulging closets of nonwearables are mute testimony to wrong fabrics, wrong patterns, and wrong styles.

8. Always wear rubbers or overshoes over your shoes when the ground is wet, snowy, or icy. Not only do they give you better traction, reducing the chance of a fall, but they keep your shoes dry. The single biggest destroyer of shoes and soles is moisture. If you get those shoes wet by walking in snow or rain, the leather will harden, the stitching will harden, and shrink, and they will destroy themselves much faster. In addition, you'll be walking around in wet shoes all day, increasing the chance of your picking up some kind of illness.

9. Buy out-of-season clothes when they are on sale, such as winter clothes and coats in the spring, and summer clothes in the fall.

10. For women, adding accessories, such as scarves and jewelry, can make something look entirely different, even though you've had it in your closet for many years. In addition, try to make sure that skirts and blouses can be interchangeable. In this way, two of each can really become four different outfits.

11. When shopping for clothes, if you find something you like, walk away from it. If after a half hour or so you decide you still want it, you can always go back after it. This helps you get away from "impulse" buying in clothing.

Clothing is one of the easiest places to overspend—and, consequently, one of the easiest to cut back. Control your impulse buying; learn that no matter how low-priced something might be, it's no bargain if you don't need it; and learn to use it up, wear it out, make it do, or do without. When you do, this part of your budget will continue to decrease.

7

How to Choose
Insurance

Sensible people will see trouble coming and avoid it, but an unthinking person will walk right into it and regret it later (Prov. 27:12).

Another living cost you can't avoid is insurance premiums.

The only way you can care for your family financially after you die is by building up assets while you are living or by purchasing life insurance. Unless you have the former, you are going to have to plan on paying premiums for the latter.

Another kind of insurance you should carry, required by law in most states, is automobile insurance, at least liability or no-fault.

If you own a home, you must also buy certain kinds of insurance on that home if it is mortgaged. The mortgage holder requires insurance to protect the asset which backs up the loan.

There are also kinds of optional insurance, which these days are barely in the optional category. Medical and hospital, major medical, and income-protection insurance are the most highly desirable of these so-called optional coverages.

Let's look at the most important types of insurance and the order in which you are most likely required to acquire them.

AUTOMOBILE INSURANCE

If you finance the purchase of a car, whoever lends you the money will require that you buy insurance on it to protect his investment. If you live in states that require you to carry automobile insurance of one kind or another, you'll also be forced to buy that before you can get a state license for your car.

Even if you buy the car for cash and live in a state with no insurance requirements, it's still extremely important that you purchase at least liability insurance on your automobile. If you were to kill or seriously injure another person, as a Christian you would have an obligation to care for that person or his survivors as long as such care was needed.

Even those not concerned for others would find it highly desirable to carry this kind of insurance, simply because if they kill or injure someone or damage their property, they can be sued, and huge judgments can be secured against them. Not too many people can write a check for such a court order, so it means they might be paying for that accident for the rest of their lives unless they carry liability and probably property-damage insurance.

Here are some tips to follow in buying automobile insurance:

- It's usually better to select insurance with a larger deductible. The insurance premiums you pay are not tax deductible, but the losses you sustain are tax deductible after the first $100. So if your deductible is larger than $100, you get at least a part of the loss back, and your premiums will be smaller.

- It's normally not advisable to file small claims, since they could increase future premiums. This is true with any kind of insurance.
- Many different kinds of automobile coverages are available, but you probably won't want to carry them all. Shop around, learn what you need, and pick and pay for only that much.
- Liability coverage that protects you from potential financial damages in the event of an accident is the most important.

Other important kinds of coverage are:

- Collision, probably required if your auto is financed, covers damages to your car resulting from an accident, including those involving an uninsured motorist or a hit-and-run driver.
- Bodily-injury liability protects you when your car is involved in an accident where a pedestrian or occupant of any vehicle involved is injured or killed. It also protects you and your family or anyone else driving your car with your permission, or the same people driving another person's car with that person's permission.
- Comprehensive physical damage covers damage to your car resulting from fire, vandalism, theft, and usually from natural catastrophes.
- Uninsured-motorist insurance covers bodily injury to any occupant of your car if you are involved in an accident with an uninsured motorist or hit-and-run driver. You and your family are also covered if you are injured in another person's car or as a pedestrian.

- |Medical payments| cover medical expenses for all
  occupants of your car resulting from accidental in-
  juries.

Select only the coverages you think you will need and
shop the market. The services of a good, reputable agent
can be extremely important to you.

LIFE INSURANCE

Life insurance is|protection,| not an investment. It is pro-
tection of your dependents against financial and economic
loss caused by death. If the breadwinner in the family
dies unexpectedly, the family will need money to cover
burial expenses, the readjustment period, living expenses,
and other funds just to keep the family together.

In addition, it is highly desirable to have enough funds
to liquidate mortgages and other debts, funds to help
educate the children, funds to make a bequest to the
work of the Lord, and perhaps even funds for your survivor's retirement expenses.

Life insurance is of two basic kinds. The first is|_term_|
life insurance. This provides protection only. Normally,
the premiums on term insurance increase as you get
older, and these increases customarily come every year
or every five years.

The way to avoid the premium increases is to use
declining term insurance. This means that for a level
premium which will never go up, the amount of the insurance drops periodically, so that at some point down
the line the insurance almost disappears. This type of
insurance may serve your family situation as your children
grow up and leave, and any remaining dependents may
have other sources of income when you get to the place
where the declining term insurance loses most of its
value.

Term insurance is the kind of insurance most highly recommended, for it does what you want life insurance to do—protect your dependents.

The second kind of life insurance is *whole life*, which goes under a number of different names. Whole life insurance provides protection plus savings. The savings then may be paid back to you in the form of *annuity payments* at some specified time in the future, usually after the age of 65, or they may be used to reduce future premiums.

In the meantime, your savings are building very slowly, and the interest rate on them is far less than you could earn elsewhere. As an investment, life insurance is poor. As protection, it is excellent. So purchase protection from an insurance company, but make your investment decisions separately.

To give you an idea of the difference in cost, in 1980 one life insurance company quoted an annual first-year premium of $117 for $50,000 in term insurance, and an annual fixed-level premium of $714 for $50,000 in ordinary or whole life insurance, for a person at the age of 30. The premiums will be higher or lower based on your age, so there is considerable leeway in the percentage of your income that should be devoted to this necessary expense.

Talk to a good Christian life-insurance agent. Tell him you want to buy protection for your family. Even though his commissions are higher on whole life insurance, he will usually recommend term insurance.

Many people ask whether or not their wives and children should be insured. If the economic loss of a working wife, for example, cannot be absorbed with your current assets or income, she should be insured. As for children, purchasing life insurance is usually a waste of money, except for funds necessary to handle burial expenses if they died prematurely.

If you are single, and have no family obligations, you probably don't need any life insurance. It is true that the longer you wait before buying even term insurance, the higher the starting premium will be; however, the number of years you don't pay any premiums at all usually more than offset the higher premiums once you start to pay them.

Life insurance is important. The breadwinner in every Christian family should carry an adequate amount of term insurance. What's adequate? Again, it depends on the size of your family, your debts, and other obligations. Sit down with your husband or wife and add up what would be needed if the breadwinner were to die within the next five years, ten years, and twenty years. It would only be an estimate, of course, but it's much better than simply picking a figure out of the air.

The average family of four will probably need at least $75,000 to $100,000 in life insurance at today's living costs. (in 1981!)

MEDICAL INSURANCE

Medical insurance is the third most desirable kind of insurance for people with dependents, and the second most desirable for single people. Hospital bills can be enormous, and you don't have to stay in for more than a few days to reach shocking heights.

If you are employed, most companies provide some kind of medical and hospitalization insurance. Your employer may pay all or part of the premium, but either way, it's a bargain for you. Group coverage is usually less expensive and group policies are usually more inclusive than individual policies.

When you select medical insurance, you have two good options. The first is to buy regular health-care insurance

When you do this, watch for exclusions. Be sure you understand the terms of the policy. Select as large a maximum benefit as possible to cover those catastrophic losses, and also try to get along with as high a deductible as you can afford to hold premium costs down. Coverages and premiums are not the same from company to company, and you can make a good buy or a poor buy in health insurance.

The second type of coverage is what is called a Health Maintenance Organization (HMO). Such an organization was first popularized by Henry Kaiser, the famous shipbuilder during World War II. Kaiser not only set up complete health care for his employees but even built hospitals for them and their dependents.

The philosophy of HMOs is preventive health care. Because you pay only one fee per month for almost every type of care you need, including physical examinations, you are more likely to have something checked out by the doctor before it requires major medical expenses.

From the doctor's side, because he is working in what is normally a larger health facility, owned and operated by the HMO, he does not have to make enormous investments in facilities and equipment, pay administrative and clerical staffs, set up laboratories, and absorb all the other overhead costs. These costs can be spread out among many doctors and many patients. Consequently, health maintenance organizations are considered a better buy than individual or group health-insurance policies.

The advantage to you, the patient, is that all your health-care needs, from routine physical exams to major surgery, are covered by that one monthly payment. Such things as the purchase of drugs can be a tremendous benefit to you, because with most HMOs all you pay is a small fee every time you need drugs for a specific illness. For example, one large HMO in the midwest has a basic charge of only

$2.50 for any drug prescription. If you have an extended illness for which drugs are needed over a period of time, this feature alone can save hundreds of dollars, and the monthly premium costs for HMO coverage is practically the same as regular health insurance.

Each time you visit the doctor while insured under one conventional health plan, you would receive a bill. If the deductible has been satisfied, you would still be obligated to pay 20% of that bill. In an HMO no bill would be sent or paid by you for a visit to your doctor. All the visits you have to make to the doctor are covered by the plan. Imagine the savings if you had to see the doctor many times in a given period.

The drawbacks are that you may not always be able to select your own doctor. If your favorite doctor does not belong to an HMO, you may have to change doctors. This is no problem for most people.

Another drawback is that HMOs are not yet available in many parts of the country, particularly in smaller communities. However, at the rate they are growing in popularity, they should soon be within easy driving distance of most Americans.

Federal law provides that if a company has 25 or more employees, it can be mandated by a *federally approved* HMO to offer the alternative. There are similar state laws for *state approved* HMOs to mandate also. However, most HMOs increase their membership through competitive marketing techniques rather than the mandating.

The laws further stipulate that an employer must pay the same amount of premium that is now in force when offering the HMO. The employee may be asked to make up the difference between what the company pays and the premium charged by the HMO. Rates may vary depending on the size of the group. Usually the larger the group, the lower the cost.

Whether you are single, married, with or without dependents, and healthy or not feeling too good, you need
some kind of health-care insurance.

HOMEOWNER'S INSURANCE

A homeowner's insurance policy is a comprehensive
policy that covers your home and its contents. You should
insure your home at its market value, and during a time of
inflation, when its value is going up, the amount of your
insurance should be increased every year. However, do
not insure the cost of the lot or approximate market
value of it. Even if your house burns to the ground, you
still have the land left.

NOTE
✗
✗

Five different forms of homeowner's policies are offered in most states. All five are divided into two separate
sections. The first section outlines the limits of the property coverages; the second, the limits of medical payments
and personal liability coverages.

One of the five standard policies is basically a renter's
policy, limited to personal property and the contents of
an apartment.

The other four are similar, except that as you go up the
scale in premiums you also have greater coverages. For
example, in the basic homeowner's policy you might not
have coverage for perils to your property from explosions,
aircraft, vehicles running into your house, falling objects,
or damage to the house from weight of ice, snow, or sleet.
More expensive policies will. Your mortgage holder requires you to have some kind of comprehensive insurance on the house itself. The amount will have to at least
equal the amount of the mortgage, and in many cases it
will be the amount of the replacement cost of your home.

If any of your contents are financed, such as your furniture or television set, the company that finances them

is also likely to want evidence of insurance on your contents. This is why a homeowner's policy is such a good investment. Rates and coverages are not identical with all insurance companies, so you will need to shop around.

Try to live with as large a deductible as you can. Premiums are not tax-deductible, but losses are tax-deductible after the first $100. Absorb those small claims as much as you can. It may help you hold down future premiums. Your insurance agent can tell you whether or not that's true with his particular company.

Finally, the service and reputation of your insurance agent is vital. A good one will be happy to give you complete details, including the advantages and disadvantages of each option.

INCOME-PROTECTION INSURANCE

The most valuable financial asset you have is your own earning power. During your lifetime, you can expect to earn more than the amount of life insurance you would ever be able to buy. Consequently, if you are unable to work because of illness or accident, you are losing your biggest financial asset.

Think what would happen to your family if the breadwinner were disabled. From a financial standpoint, disability could be more disastrous than death. The living expenses of the disabled person continue and would probably increase. In addition, the disabled person might not be able to care for himself, and, consequently, a spouse who formerly would have been able to work would likely be staying home to provide the necessary loving care and nursing services.

This is why disability income insurance is one of the most important types of optional insurance coverages.

Many people place it right behind life insurance as protection for your family and dependents.

Typically, a wage earner carrying this type of insurance will insure up to 60% of his income. It is relatively inexpensive insurance, and the proceeds are usually tax free. Some experts suggest that you select as long an *elimination period* as your personal financial reserves will allow. For example, if you do not start receiving payments for three months after being disabled, rather than one month, your annual premium is reduced by about 30%. If you can live on your own resources for six months after being disabled and write the policy accordingly, the annual premium for the one-month effective date is reduced by about 40% a year. But unless you are on a very tight budget, the relatively low cost for this type of insurance may make it better for you not to risk a long elimination period.

Select both accident and sickness disability coverage with lifetime benefits, if possible, and make sure that your policy is noncancellable and guaranteed renewable. This means the insurance company can't pull the rug out from under you by refusing to continue the insurance, and if you become partially disabled, make sure your policy permits you to engage in a different occupation from that occupation which is covered by the policy.

Income-protection insurance or disability-income insurance is vitally important even though you may receive some benefits from social security. Social security may provide a benefit; however, you must be totally and permanently disabled to qualify, and the government's definition of disability makes qualification for these payments difficult.

Check with your employer to see if some kind of group income-protection insurance is available through your company. If not, talk with your insurance agent to get the details. Those premiums could be worth far more to you than anything else with comparable cost.

OTHER KINDS OF INSURANCE

Accidental-death insurance is popular. One of the reasons is that the premiums are low and, in turn, the premiums are low because not many people die accidentally.

Special cancer insurance is becoming more popular; however, if you know what's in your medical policy and you have a good one, or if you belong to an HMO, it may be a duplication and an unnecessary expense.

The key to establishing adequate insurance protection is to acquire some knowledge in this area. Find a Christian friend or insurance agent who can help.

8

Making Your Income Stretch

> *Homes are built on the foundation of wisdom and understanding. Where there is knowledge, the rooms are furnished with valuable, beautiful things (Prov. 24:3-4).*

Malcolm MacGregor, in his book *Your Money Matters,* says you will reduce your spending by $50 to $175 per month just by keeping records. If your money is not stretching far enough, it's probably because you don't know where it's going.

It is difficult to discipline ourselves to make up a budget every month, showing exactly how much we may spend for every item of expense. And it is much tougher to stick to that budget every day. But once we learn the five magic words, "It's not in the budget," we've taken the biggest single step toward eliminating the statement, "But our income just does not stretch far enough."

If you really want to live within your income, the time to start is right now.

First, if you are borrowing money to increase your spending, and therefore not living within your income, you're not being faithful with what God has entrusted to you. That's why soldiers in Jesus' day were advised, "Be content with your pay" (Luke 3:14). One way to be unfaithful with what you have is to insist on having more by borrowing for spending. Such lack of financial management is the fastest road to financial destruction.

It is strongly recommended that you get together with your wife or husband, decide to work together to find ways to "be content with your pay," and get to work on it. You and your spouse must agree if you are going to make a budget work. If you are a single person, it requires the same degree of dedication to your financial goals.

PERSONAL FINANCIAL SUMMARY

At the end of this chapter are two forms, the first being a "Personal Financial Summary." It is for you to find out where you are financially. Fill it in by listing everything you own (section A). Start with any cash you have on hand or in your checking account (item 1). Next call your insurance agent to determine if your life insurance has any cash value; if so, fill in that line (item 2).

Then write out the total of all the savings you might have in certificates or passbook accounts in banks, savings and loans, and credit unions (item 3). Add the amount in money-market funds if you have any. If you have stocks or bonds, including U.S. Savings Bonds, fill in the present market value (item 4).

Next list the total value of all real estate you own, including your house (item 5). Put in the actual market value, based on what you think it would bring. Look at what's being asked for houses in your neighborhood. You don't have to pay for a professional appraiser to get a good idea of what your house is worth. If you own any other real estate, such as a lake cabin, an empty lot, or income property, estimate the current market value, and write that total in (item 5-6).

List all of your other investments, such as a second mortgage, contract for deed, or collectibles, in item 6.

Personal possessions come next. You'd be amazed at what it would cost to replace all the things you own if you had to buy them new. But if you bought everything used, you could probably refurnish each room in your house for about $900, on the average, including your TV set. Write in the realistic sale price in item 7.

Under item 8, list the current market value of your car(s). Your car dealer can get that information for you by looking at his car-value book.

Then list the current reasonable market value of any other property you own (item 9). Think this through carefully and list everything you own, because you probably own a good deal more equipment, stereos, fishing gear, and the rest. Put in a reasonable market value, not what you paid for it or what you hope it's worth.

Finally, under item 10, put in any "vested interest" value you have in a retirement or pension plan. This is what is actually yours right now, even though you might not be able to get it until you retire. Your employer will be happy to tell you what it is.

When you have completed these 10 items, add them up and get the grand total of everything you own, at what would be the current cash or market value. This is the value of your physical assets.

On the second part of the "Personal Financial Summary" make a list of everything you *owe* (section B).

In item 1 write in the current balance of the mortgage on your home. Then write in what you owe to others, such as the bank on a personal, automobile, or remodeling loan (item 2-a). Do the same for items 2-b and 2-c. After item 2-d list any money you might owe your insurance company for what your have borrowed against the cash value of your insurance policy. List any loans from members of the family in item 2-e.

Then list the total amount you owe on your credit cards (item 3). Some of this will be for charges made during the past 30 days, and even though it's current, it should be included. Other balances owing might be on the three-month payment plan; but whatever it is, add it all together and list it.

Anything else you owe to other businesses, such as department stores and service repair shops, should be listed in item 4. Write down what you owe to doctors, dentists, and hospitals for health care in item 5, and put down anything else you owe to anybody else in item 6.

Then add up everything you owe to others, some of which will be due at the end of the month and some of which may be a part of a 20- or 30-year mortgage on your house. Whatever it is, add up the total amount, because that's what you owe to someone else.

Finally, at the bottom of the page, fill in the Recap. List the market value of all you presently own (item A), subtract from it the amount that you presently owe (item B), and you will discover how much you are presently worth (item C). You will probably be surprised to discover that you are worth more financially than you thought.

Then write down under item D the number of years you have been at work accumulating this net worth; divide item C by item D, and you will discover how much your net worth has grown each year (item E).

You may be amazed to discover that you are worth more this year than you were last year, despite the fact that it's been a real struggle to pay the current bills as they come due. You may be doing quite well, but if not, you've taken the first step to turn things around.

Now that you know where you are, it's important to

know the direction you're heading financially. The only way to do that is to figure out how much you are receiving as income, and how much you are spending. Then you can see where changes may be needed to get your finances back under control.

INCOME AND EXPENSE STATEMENT

Part 2 of your budget preparation is listing how much you are earning and learning how much you are spending. Stop now and fill out the "Income and Expense Statement," which is at the end of this chapter.

First, list your gross income from your paycheck stubs, subtract the deductions and write in your take-home pay (MONTHLY INCOME, items 1-3). It's amazing how much of your pay is taken away before you get it!

Under Monthly Living Costs *Stewardship* is listed first, because I am convinced we should follow scriptural instructions to give God the "first fruits" of all that we earn. Your contributions to God's work are an integral part of managing your money. I highly recommend giving a full 10% (tithe) of your gross income and "turning" the rest of your finances over to God through prayer. He will make sure that all your financial necessities are met. You may not have your struggles eliminated, but with his help you will discover a way to manage your finances. (See Chapter 15 on this.)

You will probably spend between 20% and 30% of your take-home pay for *Food and Beverage* (item 2), even though most recent national studies show that the average American in 1980 spent 19.91% of take-home pay on food and drink. Obviously, if you have a large family, it will be necessary to spend more money for food than for a smaller family. However, if you are above the 30% level, you know that you are spending too much on food.

Next, fill in your *Housing Costs* (item 3). Here another big variation can take place. Studies by the U.S. Department of Commerce show that housing costs are rising at the same time that food and clothing expenses are declining as a percentage of take-home pay.

These 1978 figures show that housing cost the average family $21.89 out of every $100 of take-home pay, and it is rising steadily. On top of that, if you own your own home, there is an additional $7.91 out of each $100 for operating expenses, not including utilities. This brings the total up to $29.80. Add in heat, light, and water, and you're up to an average of $33 out of every $100. Consequently, if you are at the national average of home owners, which covers a wide range of salaries and family sizes, you are going to be spending 33% of your income on housing, if you own your own home.

You may be getting by for less, or may be spending more. If you are spending too much more than the recommended ceiling of 30%, you'll need to find out why.

Then comes *Clothing* (item 4). In 1978 U.S. Department of Commerce figures show that the average family spent 7.2% of their income for clothing. This is near the bottom of the range that we have shown. Those living in northern climates would have to spend a little more, as would those with larger families. But you should be within the range, remembering the more you spend for clothing or any other item, the less you have to spend elsewhere in your budget.

Health care (item 5), an important cost for any family, averaged out to 10.31% of the take-home pay for the average family in 1978. This is up from 8.87% in 1972 and up even further from the 6.41% of take-home pay in 1960. Your age, the size of your family, and other factors will determine where you fall in this recommended range. Include drugs in this category.

Transportation in 1978 cost the average American about $14 out of every $100 in take-home pay. You should list the amount you spend for transportation (item 6) to see how you compare. This is one of the places you may be able to cut the amount you spend to make up for what might be overpayments in some of the other categories.

Other insurance (item 7) includes life insurance, salary continuation, and any other specialized insurance that your particular circumstances make it wise for you to consider.

As we pointed out in Chapter 7, term life insurance is the one we recommend, for it's the cheapest kind. Remember that you buy life insurance to protect your survivors against financial catastrophe, particularly should you die while you still have young children at home or others who are heavily dependent on your earning power.

We have recommended that 2% to 5% of your income be set aside to purchase life insurance. Obviously, if you are a single person with no dependents, you need only enough life insurance to settle your debts, burial expenses, and other obligations should you die unexpectedly. If you have several children, you need more term life insurance, and a higher percentage of your income must be devoted to it.

Income protection insurance is particularly important if you are a relatively young person with many dependents. Every year thousands of wage earners are totally disabled and lose their single biggest financial asset—their earning power. You are already partially covered by Social Security, and if your disability is job-related, workers' compensation insurance, which is mandatory in all 50 states. However, if you want to maintain your present standard of living, you should look into the cost of carrying income protection insurance. Again, the percentage of your income you devote to this expense will depend on your present income level, the costs of supporting your family, and the difference between that cost level and what you will receive from Social Security or any other income source available to you (such as through your company hospitalization or medical plan, many of which have disability features).

Education and Recreation (item 8) comes to a total of $8.61 for the average American family, out of every $100 earned. If you cut down on toys, sporting goods, radio, TV, records, spectator amusement tickets, and even magazines which go unread, you can cut your cost of living significantly.

Finally, item 8 covers *Installment Payments* for everything except your home mortgage. Here is where many people are likely to be in trouble.

The August 6, 1979, issue of *U.S. News and World Report* stated that people used $23 of every $100 after taxes to repay their debts. This high figure puts people into a dangerous financial position. For many years we considered 15% to be the absolute maximum of your take-home pay that you could commit to repaying installment debt. In recent years, we have revised that upward to 18%, but that is a risky, absolute top level. If your installment debts add up to more than 18% of your take-home pay, you should immediately stop buying anything else on an installment basis until some of those installment contracts and loans are paid in full.

Once you get below that 15% level, do everything possible to keep it there. As inflation increases and the cost of interest for these installment payments climbs, try to get below the 10% level in installment payments. If more than $10 out of every $100 you are bringing home has to go out to repaying installment debt, you are putting yourself under a great deal of unnecessary emotional, mental, and psychological pressure.

Now add your totals and write in the grand total in item 9. The amount you spend should be the same or less than your take-home pay. If your income just does not stretch far enough, it's probably because you don't know where you are spending it.

Many who say it is impossible to get by at certain salary levels fail to recognize that others with exactly the same income and same size families are doing it.

In counseling with many people, I have noted that regardless of their income, a certain percentage of families are always in financial trouble; and regardless of the size of income or size of family, a certain percentage manages to stay out of financial trouble.

Some families earn $12,000 per year, rear four children, and pay their bills on time. Some single people who earn $12,000 a year can't seem to cover their expenses and live within their incomes. The same thing holds true at much higher income levels. Above certain bottom limits, it's not really how much you earn, but how you spend it, that determines whether you will be continuously stuck in the debt trap or financially free.

GETTING OUT OF TROUBLE

Chapter 1 described the financial hole Mary and John had dug for themselves. They were on the verge of losing all their possessions, and their young family was starting to come apart.

Was it possible for John and Mary to work themselves out of their situation? The answer is yes, but they were unusually determined. What they needed was help in learning how to spend money. As their counselor introduced them to God's ways of managing personal finances, they learned the truth of the statement, "I have the strength to face all conditions by the power that Christ gives me" (Phil. 4:13).

After John disposed of the motorcycle and the car and managed to reduce those payments through compromise arrangements, he paid off the two hospital bills and the finance company through a loan from the credit union at his place of employment. The new monthly payments were stretched out, but were much smaller.

We then had a talk with the landlord, who had prepared an eviction notice after carrying this young couple two and sometimes three months in arrears for nearly two years. By agreeing to pay $25 extra each month, and keeping that promise, they managed to catch up on their rent.

During the time it took John and Mary to work themselves out of debt, neither bought any clothing. Their families gave them and their children gifts at Christmas and their birthdays, always clothing or something equally practical.

This story has a happy ending, for at the end of two years, John and Mary were out of debt.

What do you suppose John wanted to do then? Go out and buy a new car! But after a little persuasive counseling by his wife and his financial advisor, exactly the same amount that had been going out on the credit-union loan was put into a savings account. They soon had their savings invested in a higher-yielding money-market fund, and shortly before the price of houses started to skyrocket, they had enough for a down payment on a home of their own.

John and Mary still do not have an automobile. They place a much higher priority on their home, and that decision has served them well.

Other ideas that helped John and Mary were these:

- Try not to carry anything in your purse or billfold smaller than a $20. It makes it much harder to spend money if you have to break that twenty. It's a good habit in self-discipline.

- Do without many of the things that you have taken for granted. You don't have to eat lunch every day. Your body will probably benefit from skipping lunch occasionally and will surely benefit from skipping dessert, soft drinks containing sugar, junk foods of all kinds, and even short rides in the car which could better be replaced by the healthful exercise of walking.

In many little ways you can save a dollar here and a dollar there to have a balanced budget. Then you will have to agree with Malcolm MacGregor that you will reduce your spending by $50 to $175 every month, simply by keeping records. You can do it.

PERSONAL FINANCIAL SUMMARY

Amount

A. What we own:

1. Money in checking account and cash on hand $_____
2. Cash value of life insurance   _____
3. Savings (savings & loan, credit union, bank, etc.)   _____
4. Stocks and bonds (present market value)   _____

     Total (1-4) cash and other savings: $_____

5. Real estate
    a. Home (today's market value)   _____
    b. Other real estate (cabin, lot, etc.)   _____

     Total (5) real estate: $_____

6. Other investments (collectibles, C/Ds, etc.)   _____
7. Personal possessions (use realistic sale value)   _____
8. Automobiles (average retail price)   _____
9. Other property   _____
10. Interest in retirement or pension plan   _____

     Total (6-10) other property $_____
     Grand total of what we own: (assets) $_____

Amount due

B. What we owe:

1. To the mortgagor of our home $_____
2. To others:
    a. Bank   _____
    b. Loan company   _____
    c. Credit union   _____
    d. Insurance companies   _____
    e. Family loans, etc.   _____
3. To credit card companies   _____
4. To other businesses   _____
5. For medical, dental, hospital   _____
6. Other   _____

     Grand total of what we owe: (liabilities) $_____

Recap:

A. Grand total of what we own (assets) $_____
B. Less grand total of what we owe (liabilities)   _____
C. What we have accumulated (net worth)
    (A minus B)   _____
D. Number of years of accumulation   _____
E. Average annual accumulation of resources
    (C divided by D)   _____

INCOME AND EXPENSE STATEMENT

Monthly income
1. Gross income (before deductions) $_____
2. Deductions $_____
3. Take-home pay $_____
4. Subtract total monthly living costs
   (from No. 10 below) $_____
5. Amount left over to save (or amount short) $_____

Monthly living costs	Amount you spend	Take home pay	National average for family of four
1. Stewardship (Church and other contributions)	$_____	$_____	10%
2. Food and beverage	$_____	$_____	20%-28%
3. Housing			
Rent or house payments:_____			
House operation:			
a. Gas _____ e. Repairs_____			
b. Light _____ f. Taxes _____			
c. Phone _____ g. Insurance _____			
d. Water _____ h. Other _____			
Total $_____		$_____	20%-30%
4. Clothing	$_____	$_____	7%-10%
5. Health care			
a. Physician _____			
b. Dentist _____			
c. Insurance _____			
Total $_____		$_____	8%-11%
6. Transportation (Car operating expenses, or public transportation, not including car payments)	$_____	$_____	8%-13%
7. Other insurance			
a. Term life	$_____	$_____	2%-4%
b. Salary continuation	$_____	$_____	2%-4%
8. Advancement			
a. Education _____			
b. Recreation _____			
c. Other _____			
Total $_____		$_____	4%-10%
9. Installment payments (not including home mortgage)			
a. Car payment _____			
b. TV payment _____			
c. Furniture payment _____			
d. Other loans _____ (bank, finance co., credit unions)			
Total $_____		$_____	10%-15%
10. Total monthly cost of living	$_____	$_____	100%

9

Getting
Out of Debt

Borrow money and you are the lender's slave (Prov. 22:7).

How much debt can you afford to carry? Actually you shouldn't have any debt, except for the mortgage debt on your home.

If you have to borrow money to buy a car, you are probably buying too expensive a car. Settle for a used car, and save until you have enough money to buy it.

If you have to borrow to buy furniture, you are spending too much. Borrow furniture from your family or friends until you've saved enough to buy good used furniture. Probably it will be better quality than the new furniture you have to finance, and it will be cheaper.

Occasionally you are forced into debt, such as having unexpected hospital bills not fully covered by your insurance. In these cases, where you cannot pay them off in full immediately, you will end up with an unexpected debt.

The amount of debt that Americans are committing themselves to repay has been growing steadily in recent years. One of the principal reasons is a new disease called *agoramania.*

Agoramania has been spreading across North America and part of the rest of the world. It is the compulsion to buy. Kleptomania, the compulsion to steal, has been recognized as a malady for years, but agoramania is just beginning to be noticed. It is not just an illness of individual persons, however, for the entire general public seems subject to it. Some think it is because of extensive advertising that stimulates the public to think they are not well off until they have bought a particular product.

The problem is that Americans are trying to buy the world. We already use more than 30% of the world's resources, and we buy much more as individuals than we need. It is strange how nations and individuals so rich in food and luxuries are not satisfied. We seem to equate happiness with buying, whether we need what we buy or not.

Another reason for the rapidly mounting personal debt load carried by many Americans is the buying psychology of inflation.

More and more people seem to want to buy more and more things "before the price goes up." They don't have the money to do it, so they borrow, seldom stopping to assess fully the commitments they are making, and seldom stopping to determine whether they will ever really need those things they are hurrying to buy before the price goes up. Many people trade in perfectly good automobiles, for example, that would serve them for several more years in order to buy a brand-new one "before the price goes up."

Others are buying new clothing "before the price goes up," or new television sets, washing machines, dryers, and items that are luxuries even by today's standards, such as video tape recorders for their television sets.

As a result, according to the U.S. Department of Commerce (*U.S. News and World Report,* August 6, 1979) the average American has committed 23% of his take-home pay to paying back non–real estate mortgage debt before he even gets his paycheck.

How true it is that as long as our lives are centered around the things of this world instead of being centered around the things of the Holy Spirit, we will buy ourselves into trouble. From these purchases may come the temporary joys of ownership and the temporary pleasures of use, but from them also come the long-range burdens of debt, the long-range worries of making those monthly payments, and the continuous worry of taking care of all the things we have purchased. Before we know it, we recognize that our possessions own us, and we don't really own them.

But it's too late to talk about not getting in debt. You're already in debt, and it's time to work on getting out of it. George Fooshee, the author of *You Can Be Financially Free,* talks about "Escaping the Debt Trap." Debt really is a trap, and escaping it is what you have to do if you are in it.

ESCAPING THE TRAP

You can escape that trap now if you really set your mind to it and go about it in a planned, dedicated, high-priority manner. Here are steps you can take:

1. Make a complete list of all people and institutions to whom you owe money and how much.

2. Add up those amounts so you'll have an idea of the size of the total problem.

3. Make a list of all of the monthly payments you have promised to make.

4. Add up all the monthly payments so you can see, perhaps for the first time, how much you have committed yourself to pay every 30 days.

5. Start giving a set percentage of your take-home pay to God every Sunday. Don't wait and do it once every three months or at the end of the year. (See 1 Corinthians 16:2 and Chapter 15.) It's important to make this commitment first, because you are going to ask for God's blessings on your plan to repay your debts. Make sure that God knows that you have put him first in your life. If you do, not only will you keep your promises to repay your debt, but by putting God first you will put "things" second and be able to resist the temptation to buy still more.

6. Have a garage sale. You probably have many things in your house that you do not need and never use. You might have an extra lawn mower, the snowmobile suit that no longer fits you, the three extra sets of dishes that only collect dust, that camping tent that was such a good buy but was only used twice before it went into a corner, your old set of golf clubs replaced by that new set, and many other things. When you start to clean house and move everything you have not used in the last year out to the garage, you will have quite a collection of things for sale. Estimate their value, put an ad in the paper and a homemade sign on a tree at the front of your lot, and set up shop. You'll be amazed at how much money you take in, and how much freer you will feel being rid of a lot of junk that has owned you much more than you have owned it. All cash from this sale should then be sent to your creditors to start reducing those installment debts.

7. Add no new debts under any circumstances. You must absolutely promise yourself that you will not buy anything else on any basis except cash.

8. Have a "plastic party." Take out all your credit cards; then you and your spouse sit down at the kitchen table with a pair of scissors and cut them to shreds. From now on all purchases will be made with cash, or they won't be made. If you are deeply in debt so your payments are at

or exceed the national average of 23% of take-home pay, you should be able to discipline yourself enough to set aside 25% of your take-home pay for paying installment debts. It will mean more macaroni casseroles, no vacation trip this year, no new clothes, and a heart-to-heart talk with the children about their expenses—but you can do it.

The checks should then be a proportional percentage of what you owe each creditor. For example, if you owe one of them $500 and your plan permits a payment of 5% of each indebtedness each payday, you will send that creditor $25. If you owe the next creditor $100, his 5% would be just $5 each payday. In this way you are treating them all on a fair and equal basis.

Goals are the important stimuli and incentives that enable you to do what is difficult. A person without a goal ambles nonchalantly through life, accomplishing little. But find the people who are making things happen, and you find goal setters.

10. After you have determined what your maximum effort will be, write a short note to each of your creditors, explain the predicament you are in and what you are going to do to work your way out of it. Most of them will be happy to accept your payment offer, providing you keep your promise. It is absolutely imperative that you make every single payment as planned. Once you break your word and go back on your plan, the creditors are much less likely to go along with any new proposal, and you really can't expect them to believe you after you fall behind initially and then fail to keep the new payment plan. If you break it, they are likely to turn the account over to their collection agency or their attorney, and either one will go after the full balance immediately.

11. Stick to your plan tenaciously. Remember this plan includes total abstinence from purchasing anything else, regardless of what it is. It includes keeping that payment

promise to every credit grantor meticulously. It includes keeping your family advised on the progress toward reaching your goals. You might even want to do this by posting a chart in the kitchen and making entries every payday as to how much is paid to each creditor and how much remains on the balance. It's a family project, and it's a good lesson to teach the children. If you had learned that lesson in your home, you might not have gotten into the debt trap where you now find yourself. You will continue to be a servant to the lender until you get these debts paid. Once they are paid you will once again regain your freedom. What a great feeling that's going to be! How great a day it's going to be for you and your family when you can say, "I'm now completely out of debt!"

And once you get there, stay there!

GETTING OUT — AND STAYING OUT

In Chapter 1 you read about Bill and Sally and how they had become slaves to their creditors. With their backs to the wall, they resolved to get out of debt.

It had been a long time since they had gone to church, and a spiritual vacuum contributed to "things" taking over as top priority in their lives. Too much good golfing weather came on Sunday mornings. As we talked, it became obvious that income was not their major problem. Personal priorities in life were their real problem.

Before they left my office, they started to lay out a new plan. First, they agreed to return to church on a regular basis. Then they decided to spend Sunday afternoons with one another. Next, they decided to drop their membership in the athletic club, removing the monthly dues expense and the temptation to spend more on those expensive meals.

After further discussion, Bill agreed to take the new

Cadillac back to the dealer to see if he could trade down to a less expensive make. Sally agreed to return two of the new dresses she had recently purchased but hadn't even worn.

Once they discovered how their priorities had been out of line and how they were spending hundreds of dollars a year on things which were "of this world" and of little importance to them, it was easy to decide where to cut expenses. The more important things such as their relationship, Bill's job, their home, and a reborn interest in their church rose to the top of their priority list.

They discovered that their financial problem was not really a financial problem. It was an emotional problem many people pass through during the middle years of their lives if they do not have their priorities in order. They were able to recognize it and had the Holy Spirit to help them take the steps to correct it.

This couple went even further. They still had two children in college, one a freshman and the other completing his junior year. They discovered there were scholarships available for students with high academic standings, and not all of them depended on financial need. They'd never even thought of inquiring about scholarships in the past. They thought they were making enough money to pay their own way, and that it was beneath their dignity for their children to receive educations with somebody else's money.

But their youngest daughter, with still more than three years of college ahead of her, was a brilliant student. She qualified for one of the many scholarships that go unclaimed every year, and started her sophomore year with all tuition, books, and laboratory fees paid. Her parents still had to pay board and room, but it greatly reduced her dependence on their income. This, along with the cuts in their own spending, released several thousand dollars per year, all of which they dedicated first to the Lord, by giving 10% of their income to him, and the balance to their creditors. It took them nearly two years to get their financial house in order, but by the time their daughter entered her senior year and their son was well into graduate school, they were out of debt.

Bill and Sally were "best friends" again, and better yet they had learned the real meaning of "seeking first the kingdom of God" (Matt. 6:33).

Once you have worked out your plan for getting out of debt, the old temptation to purchase this one lovely thing for the children or the coat you've always dreamed of will all come back. You know the stores encourage you to go ahead and buy, and you will be tempted to think that you owe it to yourself to have it. The temptation is to give in to pride and greed.

What will you do? What kind of choice will you make? It's at this point that you call on God for help. Alone you can't do battle with debt, but with him you will be able to resist those temptations.

You can speak to God as you would to any friend. "Lord, you know I don't have to have this; you know it would be wrong, since no matter how I try to convince myself, I can't pay for it when the bill is due. Lord, strengthen me to choose correctly, to lay it down and walk out of this department."

If you pray this way, God will answer your request immediately. What's more, the Bible is full of promises to those who say no to temptation. "You will become special to the Lord" (Deut. 4:30-31); "All will go well with you" (Deut. 5:29); "Your days will be long" (1 Kings 3:14); and "Your days shall be blessed" (James 1:25). These are only samples of the things God has in store for you, gifts that money cannot buy.

10

Inflation-Proof Investments

Plan carefully and you will have plenty; if you act too quickly, you will never have enough (Prov. 21:5).

You may hear comments like this about money: "Money may not be the most important thing in the world, but it's way ahead of whatever is in second place" "There are other things besides money, like poverty and welfare and starvation and all of that." But money does not make or break, it simply reveals us. Matthew Henry said, "There is a burden of care in getting riches, fear in keeping them, temptation in using them, guilt in abusing them, sorrow in losing them, and a burden of account at last to be given concerning them."

When inflation is pushing prices up faster than the interest rate on savings accounts, when common stock prices are unable to keep pace with inflation, and when many of the old rules for investing no longer apply, people with even a few dollars to invest or set aside for emergencies are asking what to do with them. Many options are still open, and some are new.

We need to start by remembering to trust in God more

than money. If we do this and seek investment answers prayerfully, they will become more evident to us. "Those who depend on their wealth will fall like the leaves of autumn, but the righteous will prosper like the leaves of summer" (Prov. 11:28). Accepting this, let's start by reading what God says about investing, for the Bible has many references to investments; for example, "Be wise enough not to wear yourself out trying to get rich. Your money can be gone in a flash, as if it had grown wings and flown away like an eagle" (Prov. 23:4-5).

At the same time, the Bible tells us to use what we have been given and to invest it wisely. One of the best known parables contrasts the wise with the unwise investing of money to make a point about life in the kingdom (Matt. 25:14-30). Although it primarily applies to the knowledge of Christ's gift and his teachings, the fact that Jesus used proper investing as a teaching tool emphasizes its importance. It also reveals how good stewards use wealth God has entrusted to them.

Some people think a Christian should not have an interest in money, because they believe the Bible teaches that money is the root of all evil. This, however, is a misinterpretation of God's Word and is sometimes used as an excuse for failure. The Bible does not say that money is the root of all evil; it says, "The *love* of money is a source of all kinds of evil" (1 Tim. 6:10). The root of evil has to do with your mind, not with money. It is your attitude, not your affluence, that determines the sinfulness of your life.

Don't be fooled by misinterpretations or misquotations of certain Bible passages into thinking there's something wrong with the desire to succeed financially. Many passages in the Bible speak clearly to the subject of personal prosperity. It seems that God takes a personal interest in how believers manage their income.

The Bible does criticize the rich, but specifically those

who make riches and power the most important things in their lives. The Scriptures describe wealthy men—Job, Abraham, Isaac, Jacob, Joseph, David, Solomon, Daniel, Joseph of Arimathea, Cornelius, and others—to show that it is not necessarily true that piety and poverty must go together. It is possible to be wealthy, yet be a faithful follower of God. Special temptations to substitute the false gods of wealth and power do confront the rich, however.

HOW TO SAVE MONEY

Your first investment, and it is an investment, should be in God's work.

The first 10% out of every paycheck should be given to the work of the Lord. This scriptural instruction not only teaches us to put God first in our lives (Deut. 14:23), but also carries with it the promise of blessings. Solomon wrote, "Honor the Lord by making him an offering from the best of all that your land produces. If you do, your barns will be filled with grain, and you will have too much wine to store it all (Prov. 3:9-10). We'll have more to say about tithing in Chapter 15.

Second, everyone should take the next 10% out of every paycheck and pay it to themselves. This means keeping it and not spending it. That 10% first becomes your savings, then your investment capital, then your key to bigger investments that will eventually start paying bigger dividends to you. It is permissible to live off the income from your investments, but you should never touch the investments themselves.

Many have started small. I know one man who had only $14 when he and his wife were married. Conscientiously they followed the principle of putting 10% from every paycheck into savings. Then they listened to the scriptural advice to build investments slowly and not make risky speculative investments. Twenty years later they could live comfortably off the income from their investments alone.

If you saved $1000 per year at 10% interest compounded annually, at the end of the first year you would have $1100. At the end of the fifth year you would have $6505, and at the end of 10 years you would have $16,579 in your savings reserve. You saved $10,000 in those 10 years, but because of interest being paid you could start drawing out $2000 a year in the 11th year, and every year thereafter for the next 11 years, and at the end of that time still have $10,211 left in your savings plan.

"Wise people live in wealth and luxury, but stupid people spend their money as fast as they get it" (Prov. 21:20). Let's look now at the types of savings investments.

SAVINGS PASSBOOK

Almost without exception every small investment program starts with a savings passbook account at a bank, a savings-and-loan association, or a credit union. Even though the current interest rate on savings passbooks is less than the rate of inflation, a savings passbook is still the cornerstone of any investment program. In spite of savings being the single most important step you can take on the road to financial security even in inflationary times, the savings rate in the U.S. has dwindled to 3.4% of disposable income. In an interview with *U.S. News and World Report* (February 4, 1980), Senator Lloyd Bentsen of Texas reported the U.S. figures at 3.4%, while in Japan it was 25%, and in France and Germany it was 13%.

You should deposit 10% of every one of your paychecks in your savings passbook until you get to that first $1000. The passbook interest rate was only 5.25 to 5.50% in 1980, but Congress has changed federal law to permit the gradual payment of higher interest rates on various savings accounts, including the passbook, up until 1985 when all controls on interest rates come off. But already your money is starting to work for you while you are accumulating enough to make investment with a higher return.

At the same time, while you are starting an investment program, you are building a cash reserve for those unexpected expenses. And every individual can expect to go through a period of financial famine. It is up to each of us to use the years of plenty to prepare for that emergency.

This is similar to the advice Joseph gave to the Egyptian pharaoh: "Now you should choose some man with wisdom and insight and put him in charge of the country. You must also appoint other officials and take a fifth of the crops during the seven years of plenty. Order them to collect all the food during the good years that are coming, and give them authority to store up grain in the cities and guard it. The food will be a reserve supply for the country during the seven years of famine which are going to come on Egypt. In this way the people will not starve" (Gen. 41:33-36).

Your famine may be a medical emergency, temporary job loss, loss of overtime, loss of one salary if a married couple are both working, moving charges, and any one of numerous other unexpected expenses. They may be unexpected, but they are not unplanned for if you have a passbook account with some readily available cash in it.

Normally, you would not touch this cash for emergencies, except as a last resort. To build your investment program you have to treat that cash as if it were not there. Once you start to dip into it for real emergencies, you'll find yourself dipping into it more and more frequently for supposed emergencies.

Most banks and savings and loans offer a wide variety of savings certificates and other options. However, few of them are really good investments in a time of inflation. For example, you may buy a four-year savings certificate that will currently yield 7.51% at a bank and .25% higher at a savings and loan. Those were good investment alternatives a few years ago, but with increased interest rates on other investment possibilities, tying your money up for four years at 7.5% makes sense only as protection against depression-lowered interest rates.

On January 1, 1980, the U.S. Treasury Department announced that banks and savings and loans could issue a new type of *small saver certificate* which carried an interest rate linked to the average two-and-a-half-year U.S. Treasury securities yield in existence at the time the certificates are issued. These new certificates run for two and a half years, pay a varying amount, currently around 10% interest with no minimum amount required to purchase one. This is another effort by the federal government to change the rules under which thrift institutions can pay depositors.

The important thing is to be aware that savings plans are changing frequently and, regardless of which plan is best for you at the moment, it is vital that 10% of your income go into savings.

Once you accumulate your first $1000 in your passbook account, you are ready for the second step. Here the return on your investment can start to gain on inflation.

The chart at the end of this chapter shows the savings options currently offered by one bank.

All savings interest rates were formerly set by the Federal Reserve Board under a law called Regulation Q. But the savings interest rates will be going up, starting in 1981, under that federal law passed in 1980. That law provides for gradual increases in all savings rates over a period of six years, until federal regulation is removed altogether, and interest rates are then set by the banks and savings and loan associations through open-market competition among themselves for your savings dollar. By that time they could, and probably will, fluctuate up and down. Because of the publicity and advertising, you'll be able to keep abreast of these changes and get the highest interest rate possible while working toward your other goals.

The new law also permits federally chartered credit unions to raise their maximum loan rates from 12% to 15%—and to issue credit cards.

Another change in federal law, which went into effect on December 31, 1980, permits banks to pay interest on checking accounts. The terms and conditions vary, but many banks require you to keep a certain minimum in your checking account (commonly $1000) before you earn interest on that money. In addition, if you fall below that minimum at any time, the banks are likely to levy penalty charges of approximately $10 per month. So, although interest on checking accounts will be hailed as a great advance for the consumer, there will be terms and conditions that will limit the real benefit from it to a relatively small percentage of the population. But it's something to ask about, as it usually includes other benefits like a free safe deposit box and free travelers checks.

MONEY-MARKET MUTUAL FUNDS

Money-market funds were started in the mid-1970s by brokerage houses that specialize in buying and selling stocks and bonds. The reason was that when stockholders sold stock, the money would simply sit in the broker's bank account, unused, until the investor decided to buy more stock. While the investor was looking around for a new stock to buy, he drew no interest on that account and, consequently, more and more investors were pulling the money out to buy short-term savings certificates at banks, or to try to put it to work in other ways.

Brokers came up with the idea of paying interest on that money while it was in the brokerage house. That kept the investors happy during periods when they had uninvested money sitting there and, at the same time, assured the brokerage house that the investor would more than likely reinvest his money in stocks and bonds, thus earning commissions for the broker. The three largest money-market funds are Merrill, Lynch, Ready Assets of New York; Dryfus Liquid Assets of New York; and Fidelity Daily Income Trust of Boston.

Since then insurance companies and banks have started their own money-market funds. These funds pool money from many investors to buy money-market instruments, short-term securities issued by banks, corporations, and the federal government at minimums, typically $100,000—well beyond the means of the average investor. With most money-market funds, there is virtually no risk of loss.

Another advantage is that you can withdraw any or all of your money from the fund at any time. It's not like buying a certificate of deposit for six months, or a bank investor's certificate for 90 days. You can simply leave your money in the fund for two or three days and draw it out, but still earn interest for those two or three days.

A third advantage is that the money-market funds have a relatively high yield, in 1980 between 8% and 17%.

A fourth advantage is that most brokerage houses, insurance companies, and banks do not charge for handling your money in these funds. That may eventually change because more and more people have learned of their existence and, instead of their simply being a depository for money temporarily uninvested by those who buy and sell stocks, they are becoming a popular investment.

Most money-market funds require a $1000 minimum deposit, and you may make additional deposits to the account at any time, with a usual minimum of $100, although some brokerage houses and banks have minimum additions of $500. It's a good investment of relatively small amounts of money for those who might need their money back on short notice and who want to draw interest well above a bank passbook savings account. However, there's one caution. A number of brokerage houses, banks, and insurance companies have gone broke over the years, and your money could go down with them. Be careful to deal only with brokerage houses insured by the Securities Investors Protective Corporation, of which there are many. The banks, of course, are covered by FDIC, and your savings are protected up to $100,000.

Typical features of insurance company money-market funds are a minimum investment of $2500, minimum withdrawals of $500, good security on your principal, and a yield of between 8% and 17% in 1980.

The $500 figure is the minimum for writing a check against the account, but you may withdraw your money at any time without loss of interest. Check with your insurance man, your broker, or your banker to learn more about money-market funds.

U.S. TREASURY BONDS, CERTIFICATES, AND NOTES

Another excellent investment after you've accumulated your first $1000 is to lend that $1000 to the U.S. Government. All you have to do is go to your own bank or brokerage house and ask one of the officers to show you a list of the "U.S. Treasury Bonds, Certificates, and Notes" that are available today, their current price, their current yield, the amount of investment required, and the date when they mature.

The list will show investments such as "Federal Home Loan Bank Bonds," "Federal Land Bank Bonds," "Federal Farm Credit Banks Consolidated Systemwide Bonds," and others. It will show how much you have to pay to buy each of the bonds, the date on which they mature, and how much interest they yield. You can buy many of these bonds in denominations as low as $1000. The maturity date (which is the date when you would get your money back at full face value plus interest) can be as close as only a few days away, or as far as 15 years or more. If the maturity is more than one year away, you receive interest payments twice each year.

If you are buying this government paper from a bank that does not have "investment trust powers," as is true with many smaller and branch banks, they will probably charge you a one-time service charge of $20 to buy each bond or note. Obviously, if you are investing $1000 for just 60 days at a 10% annual return (which would give you a 60-day return of only $16.66 less charges), it wouldn't pay you to purchase the bond through a bank without those investment powers. You'd be ahead to leave the money in your savings passbook. Generally, if you go to a bank which has investment trust powers, the fee is cut in half, or to about $10, because less paperwork is involved.

But there is a way you can buy the government paper with no commission or brokerage fee involved. Go straight to your local Federal Reserve Bank if there is one in your city. At their investment window they will take your money and give you your investment certificate, bond, or note which is due in 60 days (or whatever length of time you select), and you'll earn the full 10%, or whatever is the current interest on it.

This kind of investing is probably the second-best investment for most smaller investors today, once you put together your first $1000. You are not tied to a six-month, or longer, maturity date, as you would be if you invested your $1000 in a savings certificate with a bank or savings and loan. You can invest your money in this government paper for just a few weeks, or a few months, or until exactly the time when you are going to need it. In addition, the interest earned on many of the federal notes, bonds, and certificates of this type is not usually taxable on your state income taxes, though it is taxed by the federal government. This alone gives you an extra return on your money.

Check with your local bank or Federal Reserve office nearest you, get a copy of their latest daily listing of "U.S. Treasury Bonds, Certificates, and Notes," and read it carefully. You'll be surprised how easy it is, how flexible it is, and how great a return you can get with security.

Be careful not to purchase government paper with maturity dates that are too far away, unless interest rates are at an all-time record high and are likely to drop. The market fluctuates on these government certificates and notes, as it does on stocks. If you hold your note to maturity, you'll get back exactly what the face value says; however, if you are forced to sell it before the maturity date, it might be at a time when the value of your note or certificate has decreased (because interest rates had increased above the face interest rate of your note, making it less attractive). However, if you buy a note that matures in six months, you might find that at the end of six months, interest rates have dropped, and when you reinvest that money you'll get a lower return on it. It's better to be safe and sure when you are investing, especially when the investment represents most of your liquid cash reserves. Keep your investment in short-maturity certificates and notes. That way you'll not lose any money if you are forced to cash your note in, and it will always be available within a relatively short period of time.

Investing in U.S. Treasury Bonds, Certificates, and Notes is worth a good look, and your banker, broker, or savings and loan customer service representative will be happy to go over it in detail.

Near the bottom of the Bank Savings Chart at the end of this chapter, you will see a category called Investors Certificates, which are also sometimes called Treasury Certificates or other similar names.

These have a yield similar to money-market funds, but usually just a little lower. However, the interest rate on these certificates is guaranteed, while on the money-market funds it can fluctuate and is not guaranteed at a specific level.

The normal minimum amount you must have accumulated in order to purchase six-month bank or savings-and-loan investor certificates is currently $10,000. The interest is pegged to the interest paid by the federal government on their Treasury bills, 8% to 17% in 1980.

However, because of a new federal law, you now do not need the full $10,000 all by yourself. Since mid-1979, smaller savers have been allowed to pool their funds to meet the $10,000 minimum, but most banks don't advertise this fact because of the potential for some confusion. Call your bank and ask about plans to pool your first $1000 in savings with those of others to reach that $10,000 minimum figure. If you get 11% interest at the end of the first six months, your $1000 will have grown to $1055, and at the end of the first year to $1110.

In the meantime, you'll be continuing to set aside 10% of each week's paycheck in your savings passbook account, working toward building up that second $1000. By doing this, you are recreating your emergency fund and won't have to dip into your $1000 base investment fund, now earning 11% (more or less) in a money-market fund, a U.S. government note, or an investors certificate. When you build up just $500 this time, you can add it to your money-market fund. Or add $1000 to any of these three different good interest-yielding investments, or you can select a second one, as you start to diversify.

As your savings program grows, you will always have a little money in your passbook account. Even when you go past the $500 mark the second time and have another block of funds to invest, you will still have a few dollars left in your passbook to start to rebuild it again out of your next paycheck.

You will also pay more attention to the liquidity of your savings instruments. If you put your money into investors certificates, it is tied up for six months, unless you want to take a penalty equal roughly to one-half the interest rate. When you do that, you lose your advantage of being in an investors' certificate, but at least your money is readily available if you really need it.

If you buy a government security, and want to sell it before its maturity date, you also have to recognize that there is a market for them, which may cause the prices to go up or down almost daily. If you have to sell before the maturity date, you might find yourself getting back a little less, or possibly more, than you put in.

The money-market fund also has your money available immediately. There's no risk of any loss of the amount you put in, but the risk here is that the interest rate is not guaranteed as it is with the investors certificate and the government notes.

All three of these investments are roughly comparable as far as yield is concerned, and all three have relatively minor advantages or disadvantages. For the average beginning saver, all three are excellent second savings steps once that passbook is established.

COMMON STOCKS

As a small investor, once you have a reasonable amount of cash reserves in some sort of a savings fund or government note yielding 10% to 11%, or more, and in a form that is readily liquid, and once you have purchased a home or a condominium (Chapter 2), then you can turn to some other kind of investment. That next step could be to purchase some top-grade "blue chip" stocks.

In 1980 the dividend percentage yield on many blue chips, which fluctuate relatively little with short-term stock price and dividend changes, but still have had good long-term records, was above 8%. These include such stocks as:

Boston Edison—11.2%
Virginia Electric Power—11.1%
General Motors—10.5%
Mid-South Utilities—12.4%
Carolina Power and Electric—11.0%
New England Electric—10.4%
Southern California Edison—10.6%
Northern Indiana P. S.—9.4%
General Telephone & Electronics—9.2%
Washington Power & Water—9.1%
American Telephone & Telegraph—9.5%
Florida Power & Light—9.8%
Cincinnati Bell—8.5%
Associated Dry Goods—8.3%
Mid-Continent Telephone—9.2%

Although automobile stocks were hit hard in 1980, showing the risk of buying common stocks in even the "blue chippers," you can see how well utilities stocks perform as dividend-bearing investments. There are several in the list above.

If you are a small investor with still limited savings to invest, buy not more than 10-20 shares of any one of these stocks. This permits you to diversify your investments and hold down the 1.5% to 2.5% commission charged by most brokerage houses.

Once you get some of this stock (at the minimum commission, which might be $25), you can enroll in what is called an automatic dividend reinvestment program, which some companies offer. These have two features. First, the company will keep all the dividends that would normally come to you in small checks every three months and reinvest them in more stock at the then current market price. After the first quarter, instead of having 10 shares of stock, you might end up by having $10^{1}/_{4}$ shares. At the end of the second quarter, you might own $10^{1}/_{2}$ shares, simply because the dividends are retained by the company and automatically used to buy more stock for you.

The second advantage of the automatic dividend reinvestment plan is that you can add more money to it without paying a brokerage commission. Consequently, if you want to invest an additional $100 or $200 every month or every quarter (depending on the company's policy for their dividend reinvestment plan), you may do so by paying only a minimal service charge.

It's a great "savings account" once you get it going, and an additional plus is that the first $200 of dividends an individual ($400 for a couple filing jointly) receives each year is exempt from federal income taxes (for 1981 and 1982, and expected to be extended by Congress).

Remember, no matter how good the stock is, it may fluctuate in the short run, but in most cases will gain value over an extended period. This is why your investment in high-quality stocks, with high dividends and a history of good growth, is an excellent third step, after you have set up your savings passbook and your higher-yield savings investments. The only other third step that would precede buying stocks would be if you elected to buy a home or condominium rather than rent one (Chapter 2) or purchasing second mortgages or contracts for deed (Chapter 11).

MUTUAL STOCK FUNDS

Purchasing shares in a mutual fund is similar to purchasing shares in individual corporations. The difference is that for some of them you pay a much higher broker's or salesman's commission, usually about $8^{1}/_{2}\%$. This commission is called *loading*. There are also *no-load* funds that charge no initial commission but make their money by taking a portion of the earnings of the fund, and sometimes a selling fee when you leave. The money you invest is joined together with that of many other people and used to purchase various stocks and bonds.

Some mutual funds are speculative in nature. This means they purchase stocks they think are going to rise rapidly in market price. However, whenever you have a chance of a rapid rise, you also have a chance of a rapid loss.

Other mutual funds, called *growth funds,* invest your money in solid companies with long-term, but usually slower, growth prospects. It's a more conservative investment, and carries a lower risk of loss.

For small investors who want to spread their stock investment over a number of different stocks, and want "experts" to handle their money, mutual funds might be worth looking into. Shares in most of them can be bought and sold at will, with the minimum investment as small as $25, up to $1000 or more.

The disadvantage is the heavy "loading" or commission fees that come out of every investment you make in many of the funds. This is why there are better alternatives for most small investors. A stock brokerage firm will be happy to explain several other kinds of mutual-investment funds. The investments discussed briefly in this chapter are within the reach of every single wage and salary earner.

If you avoid being panicked by inflation into spending all your income, and patiently set aside 10% of every paycheck, you will establish a habit that will serve you well throughout your life.

BANK SAVINGS OPTIONS OPEN TO INDIVIDUALS *

Regular savings	Annual interest rate	Annual yield	Compounding	Minimum deposit
Passbook savings	5.25%	5.35%	Quarterly	No minimum
Statement savings	5.25%	5.39%	Daily	No minimum

Savings certificates

	Annual interest rate	Annual yield	Compounding	Minimum deposit
3-Mo. certificate	5.50%	5.65%	Daily	$100
1-Yr. certificate	6.00%	6.18%	Daily	$100
2$\frac{1}{2}$-Yr. certificate	6.50%	6.71%	Daily	$100
4-Yr. certificate	7.25%	7.51%	Daily	$500
6-Yr. certificate	7.50%	7.78%	Daily	$500
8-Yr. certificate	7.75%	8.05%	Daily	$500

"Investor" certificates

26-week investor certificate	Interest rate changes weekly. See your banker for the current rate. Federal regulations prohibit the compounding of interest during the term of the certificate (running 8% to 17% in 1980).		$10,000
4-yr. investor certificate	Interest rate changes monthly. See your banker for the current rate.	Continuous	Qualifying deposit required

* New law permitting higher interest rates became effective January 1, 1980.

11

More Advanced
Investments

*A good man's words will benefit
many people, but you can kill
yourself with stupidity (Prov.
10:21).*

As your financial position improves, you will first want
to consider increasing your giving from the basic 10%
of your income to a higher figure. Many Christians count
it a privilege to be able to contribute far more than a
tithe, and a few even give half of all they earn to the
work of the Lord. "Do not store up riches for yourselves
here on earth, where moths and rust destroy, and robbers
break in and steal. Instead, store up riches for yourselves
in heaven, where moths and rust cannot destroy, and
robbers cannot break in and steal. For your heart will
always be where your riches are" (Matt. 6:19-21).

One friend invests the savings God has entrusted to
him in a variety of potential profit-making ventures.
Whenever he makes a profit, he gives 100% of that profit
for God's work. It's amazing how often his investments
yield far more than he expected.

The typical successful person spends about 3000 hours
per year earning income, but only 10 hours per year on his

personal financial planning, according to Tom R. Power, president of Funds, Inc., an investment advisory firm.

As you consider the alternatives described in this chapter, remember that the greater the potential reward, the greater chance there is for a loss.

CONTRACTS FOR DEED AND SECOND MORTGAGES

The high price of houses has made second mortgages and contracts for deed (C/D, a similar borrowing "instrument" available in some states), both respected borrowing alternatives, more prevalent than ever.

If a couple wanted to sell a $75,000 house on which they had a $20,000 low-interest mortgage and the buyer wanted to assume the $20,000 mortgage, he has to come up with $55,000 in cash.

If the sellers do not need all of their cash immediately, and this is true of many elderly people selling their homes, they may be willing to take a much smaller down payment and carry the difference themselves. That difference becomes a second mortgage or a C/D. In the example above, the buyers only had $10,000 cash. The sellers were willing to accept that $10,000 as the cash down payment and let the buyers assume the $20,000, 7% existing mortgage. This left a $45,000 gap between what was paid and assumed and the purchase price. That gap was written up into a C/D, which is really a promissory note guaranteed by the real estate, signed by the buyers and sellers.

The new owners now have two payments to make. One is on the old low-interest $20,000 mortgage and the other on the C/D. Payments on C/Ds are typically 1% per month of the original balance. On a $45,000 contract, the typical provision would be for a monthly payment of

$450, including principal and interest, although they could be much lower.

C/Ds run for shorter periods of time than do first mortgages. The most common period of time is five years. This means that a great deal of it will remain unpaid at the end of five years, and will come due in a lump sum or "balloon" payment at that time.

When you purchase a home with the aid of a regular first mortgage, it is usually taken out through a savings-and-loan association or bank (or sometimes through a mortgage banker who is usually a middleman helping insurance companies and others invest their surplus cash). The title to the property goes directly to you, and you hold it in your own name. Most state laws give you an extended period to make good on any delayed mortgage payments. For example, in Minnesota you have six months to make good on past-due mortgage payments before the bank or savings and loan can start foreclosure proceedings.

On the other hand, if you buy a house with a mortgage on it, and the seller agrees to finance part of the purchase by making up the difference between your down payment and the mortgage by carrying a contract for deed or second mortgage himself, the title normally remains with the seller. You are technically the owner and live in the house, but the title remains with the person who helped you buy it by carrying the difference between your down payment and the old existing mortgage. As he still holds title to your house, some state laws provide that if you are only 60 days delinquent in your payment, the contract for deed or second mortgage holder (depending on your particular state law) can start foreclosure proceedings. Those proceedings normally take 30 days. This means that if you miss a payment, you can be evicted in 90 days if you purchase a house under the contract for deed or similar arrangement in your state.

During 1980 when mortgage money was almost impossible to find and extremely expensive when you did find it, more and more sellers helped buyers purchase their home by continuing to carry part of the financing. It's a good method to help you get into the house if you don't commit more of your income to the two payments (the first mortgage plus the contract for deed or second mortgage) than is recommended. Be sure you know what you're getting into by consulting with your lawyer or your real estate agent; both should explain things very carefully before you make the deal.

Investors come into the picture when the sellers who have taken the C/Ds (or second mortgage) instead of cash for their equity suddenly want to cash out. When they do, they will sell their C/D at a discount—15% to 25% is common. On properties where the purchaser has made a very small cash down payment (say $1000 on a $50,000 property), the C/D might be discounted up to 40%, since the buyer has little to lose by walking away from the property, and the C/D holder may find himself in possession of the house again, but in a damaged and run-down condition.

During 1980 most investors could purchase good C/Ds or second mortgages so that they were getting a yield of 20%, and sometimes more, from investments in discounted C/Ds or second mortgages. (A good C/D means that the buyer of the house had made a substantial down payment and had a big enough equity in the house so that any downturn in the economy would not likely wipe out his equity, and so cut into the C/D or second mortgage.) The term yield refers to the actual cash you are getting, related to the amount of money you have invested. So even though your C/D may have a face interest rate of only 8%, if you buy it at a price 30% lower than the face value (which is the amount upon which the 8% is being levied) the interest rate you receive (the yield) is substantially higher.

But a good, solid C/D, which was written for a good buyer who made a good down payment and, consequently, has a big equity that he doesn't want to lose, is an excellent and usually secure investment. With a discount of 20% to 25% and an interest rate around 8% (well below the commercial market), it is not difficult to have a net return of 15% to 20% on your investment. That's the monthly return in interest alone, and you'll get an additional return when the remaining face value of the C/D or second mortgage comes due.

In Chapter 1, we told about a couple who wanted to take part of their equity out of their home and invest it. We pointed out that there were no savings plans or any U.S. government securities that would have yielded enough to cover even the cost of the mortgage money they would have to borrow to get part of their equity out of their house.

We suggested that they could buy some common stock. If the price went up and was added to the dividends, they just might get 13% or more return on their borrowed equity so they would come out ahead. But nobody can count on the stock market going up. Most other kinds of investments would be ruled out because they are too risky.

But purchasing second mortgages or C/Ds is one place where they could very well use part of their current home equity wisely.

Instead of taking out a whole new mortgage, they could use a second mortgage or C/D to get some investment capital out of their house. In our example of the $75,000 home with the $20,000 mortgage, they should be able to get a $20,000 (or more) second mortgage easily. They will likely pay 12% interest (or more) on the second mortgage, but the 7% first mortgage will remain untouched.

Then by taking that $20,000 and buying at least two different C/Ds, preferably from reputable real-estate companies who handle the sale of the properties and had taken in the C/Ds as a part of the transaction, they should be able to get themselves a yield of at least 18%. This means they can keep the difference between 12% and 18% and start putting it into savings to build up another investment nest egg. If they spend the 6% spread, they might as well forget the whole thing and keep the safe equity in their house.

Terry Bates, the recent widow, whose question was described in Chapter 1, was better informed than most people. She was familiar with C/Ds or second mortgages.

Terry also knew that the interest rates on the C/Ds (or second mortgages) would be greater than the 6½% she was receiving, probably a minimum of 10%. She also knew that many sellers and real-estate brokers would accept C/Ds from purchasers of homes in order to close the deal, and would then discount them.

Terry found a $12,000 C/D carrying 8% interest at a 25% discount. She ended up with a piece of paper with an eventual value of $12,000, but having been discounted 25% cost her only $9000.

However, the 8% interest is figured on the full $12,000 face value of the C/D. This means she is getting not 8% return on her $9000 cash investment, but 8% on $12,000 —$960 per year, which is 10.6% on her $9000, and she is getting it every month with the principal and interest payment. This almost keeps her even with inflation, and she will rebuild her savings. In addition, she has a big bonus coming down the line. At the end of three years, in which the entire balance remaining on the original $12,000 is due and payable, she will receive approximately $11,000, the remaining unpaid principal.

In that three-year period, she will stay close to inflation through the interest, be building up her savings reserve because she won't spend a penny of the monthly payments she receives, and will get back her $9000 plus about $2000 cash, the remaining total of the original $12,000.

A rough calculation tells us that the interest and principal payments over that three-year period will bring her $9,000 investment up to $14,000 before taxes. Terry has been patient, has invested carefully, and has done well.

As with every other investment, there is a risk in buying second mortgages or C/Ds. But the risk is lessened if the purchaser of the property originally made a sizeable down payment, and if the contract is "cured" by having had several payments made on it while it was in the hands of the real-estate company or other investor. It is usually a safe as well as profitable place to invest excess capital, especially with home values rising steadily.

LIFE INSURANCE

Life insurance is really protection for your survivors, and should be treated as such. However, life insurance companies would also like to have you consider life insurance to be an investment. Some types of policies can serve that purpose, but the rate of return is so low, and the cost so high, that it's a poor investment.

A 1978 Federal Trade Commission report claimed that the savings component of "ordinary" life insurance in 1977 yielded only 1.3%, far below the return even on low-interest passbook savings accounts. The life insurance companies would counter by saying that some return is better than none at all, and that if you weren't compelled to pay your life-insurance premium bills every year, you wouldn't put anything into savings. They might be right, but let's hope most people have better discipline than that.

As an investment, life insurance is a poor one. Most can do better with their investment money.

ANNUITIES

Some people confuse annuities with life insurance policies, since insurance companies and brokerage houses sell both. The difference between a life insurance policy and an annuity contract is this: a life insurance policy promises to pay your beneficiaries a certain sum at your death. An annuity contract promises to pay you income while you live.

Annuities come in many forms but there are two basic types. One is called a fixed-dollar annuity, the other a variable annuity. The fixed-dollar annuity provides for a predetermined unchanging income at the time you retire or the time the annuity is scheduled to start making payments to you. The money paid by you, the annuity contract-holder, is invested in bonds and mortgages with a guaranteed return.

Under the variable annuity, the money paid in by you, at least in the past, has been invested primarily in the stock market. Real estate is becoming more popular in recent years. The income you receive varies with the investment results. The variable annuity is designed to provide a hedge against inflation, since real-estate prices and stock-market values are supposed to rise with increases in the cost of living.

You pay for annuities in two ways. The first is the *single-premium deferred annuity* which requires one lump-sum payment from you. You get it back, with interest, in a lump sum or in monthly payments whenever they are planned to start, usually as a part of your retirement plan.

The second is called a *regular deferred annuity*. You buy it by making annual installment payments over the years before retirement, then start to receive the income immediately after the last payment is made, or whenever you have predetermined to receive it.

Because your money is invested, whether you pay over the years or make a one-time payment, it earns interest, and that interest accrues to the amount that will eventually be paid to you. So an annuity for most people is an investment plan that is, in effect, a combination retirement plan and a savings plan.

An annuity does have both advantages and disadvantages, one of the latter being the sales or commission cost you pay when you purchase the annuity, and which you continue to pay as a management fee to whoever manages the investment for you. Another possible disadvantage is the lack of a guaranteed return. Some currently guarantee a return of 9% the first year, but only guarantee 3% thereafter, although they expect to do better. Although purchasing an annuity with annual, semiannual, or quarterly payments is something like putting your money into a savings account, for most people it's purchasing a regular retirement income, more than it is participating in an active investment program to stay ahead of inflation.

Annuities can, however, also be good short-term investments, if handled properly.

For example, you may be able to borrow 100% of the

cost of an annuity from a bank, at an interest rate of say 11%. Then, by shopping around, you can purchase an annuity with a yield of 11%. Consequently, your investment is fully "leverage" in that you have none of your own money invested, and the interest you are paying at the bank is covered.

You benefit from it because the interest you are paying at the bank is an expense that can be deducted from your income through other sources before paying taxes. In addition, the 11% you are earning on your annuity is tax-free income.

Many short-term annuities will give a guaranteed rate of return for six months or one year, or perhaps longer. At the same time, the interest rates you are paying at the bank can be guaranteed if the loan is written in that way —or it can be a floating interest rate tied to something like the prime rate or some other economic factor. When it is a floating interest rate, it may go down, thus increasing your yield from the annuity investment—or it may go up, decreasing your yield.

When the period during which the interest rate on your annuity expires, usually the end of six months or one year, you then have the option of cashing it in and taking the money to purchase a new annuity with the best possible yield. Your stockbroker or insurance man can advise you on which ones are giving the best yield. If you invest the interest earned on your first annuity, you do not have to pay taxes on it. However, if you keep the interest, that income becomes taxable.

Annuities are worth learning more about. They could become a good investment as well as a good savings vehicle. Talk to an expert. They'd be happy to advise you.

Money left in annuities, incidentally, is inheritance-tax free. It bypasses the probate court procedure.

TAX-DEFERRED ANNUITIES

You may be able to save several hundred dollars on your annual income-tax bill by buying a tax-deferred annuity. This savings could come from what might be called a tax loophole for the average American. It is designed to provide an incentive for families to set up their own individual retirement plans. The law provides several arrangements for allowing people to trade payment of current income taxes for a personal commitment to a personal retirement plan. These arrangements are technically known as *tax-deferred plans,* also called *tax-qualified* or *tax-sheltered plans.*

Three principal arrangements can be made: the first is called TSA (for tax sheltered annuity), the second is called HR-10 (or Keogh Plan), and the third IRA (for Individual Retirement Arrangement). They all operate on the same basic principal of tax incentives, but each has different eligibility requirements, limitations, and specifications.

TSA is for teachers, pastors, and other persons employed by certain nonprofit organizations.

HR-10 is for doctors, lawyers, farmers, small businessmen and other self-employed individuals.

IRA is for working people who are not currently included in a qualified retirement plan.

The way the plans work is to permit you to set aside a certain amount of your income in savings each year and thereby "shelter" that income from taxes during that year. Rules govern how the money is set aside and invested, and most banks and brokerage houses will be pleased to supply you with details.

If you fall into any of the categories covered by TSAs, HR-10s, or IRAs, this could be an excellent opportunity for you to investigate.

MUNICIPAL BONDS

Almost all government entities, including school districts, municipalities, watershed and park districts, finance construction and capital improvements by borrowing money. They usually borrow their money by selling bonds.

The big appeal of municipal bonds issued by the various state and local government agencies is that the interest is exempt from federal income taxes and often from state and local taxes too. The catch is that these bonds, usually sold in denominations of $5000, pay considerably less interest than taxable bonds. In 1980, for example, top-rated municipals were paying around 7%. As a general rule, you get a higher after-tax return on taxable bonds, unless your tax bracket is at least 37% (taxable income of around $30,000 for a married couple filing jointly on a federal tax return).

This is another possible investment you might want to look into, particularly if you are nearing a high income bracket. Call a stock-and-bond broker for advice.

TAX-EXEMPT BOND FUNDS

If you are in a high tax bracket, municipal bonds are a good investment because they can be exempt from both state and federal income taxes. However even they aren't foolproof. People who bought bonds in the municipalities of New York City and Cleveland learned that when they "defaulted" on payments in the late 1970s. Other government entities have defaulted on their bonds over the years, so they're not 100% risk free.

To help overcome this small risk and take advantage of changing interest rates, a number of tax-exempt bond funds have been set up. You simply invest your money in the fund, and those who manage the fund buy tax-exempt bonds from many different government entities. This way, if one of them does go bad, you stand to lose very little.

You get interest on your investment—monthly, quarterly, or semiannually, whichever you elect—but you do not report it on your tax statements.

However if your tax rate is lower than 37%, it's probably not worth your time to check these out. But if you're above it, you may want to talk to a stockbroker to learn more. Ask about the no-load funds. They have no up-front sales commission.

CORPORATE BONDS

To raise money for expansion and operating purposes, large and small corporations frequently sell bonds in multiples of $1000. These bonds also have both advantages and disadvantages.

The advantage is that the yield is usually higher than on U.S. Treasury bonds, and the money is usually secure. In addition, you will receive semiannual or sometimes monthly interest checks, so there is a relatively steady income for you.

On the negative side, most corporate bonds run for a good number of years; 10 to 40 years is the usual range. You can sell your corporate bond shortly after you buy it, but you do so at the market rate, and the market rate may be up or it may be down, depending on general interest rates.

For example, it is not uncommon for a good grade corporate bond to come out with a 12% interest rate and require a $2000 minimum investment. These would likely run for 30 years. If the interest rate on new corporate bonds coming out next year drops down to 10%, your corporate bond yielding 12% is worth considerably more because it has a better yield. Consequently the $2000 you invested might be worth $2240, and you could sell it for that amount.

But similarly, if the interest rates on the bonds coming out next year were 13% or 14%, and yours is only 12%, you'd have to discount your bond or sell it for less than $2000, maybe $1900, if you needed the cash.

One of the interesting new features in at least one corporate bond is that the corporation guarantees to pay the face value of the bond if the holder dies. This is a fairly attractive investment, then, for retired people. They can invest substantial amounts of money, get regular monthly interest checks at a good interest rate, and know that their investment (usually limited to $25,000) will be paid to their heirs in full, even though the price of their bond may have dropped.

See your broker about corporate bonds. You might buy some that were issued 27 years ago and will mature in just three years. If they were issued that long ago, they'll be selling for well below cost or *par,* because the interest rate is likely to be only 4% or 5%. But because you buy them so cheaply, the yield to you will be right around that 12% figure, and you'll soon be approaching the time when you can cash them in at face or par value.

INVESTING IN COLLECTIBLES

Because "things" go up in price in times of inflation, and cash goes down in value (purchasing power), some people are saving money by buying what are called *collectibles.* These are items that usually do not depreciate (as does a refrigerator or washing machine), but rather grow in value. They grow in value because they are scarce, and when more people want them, they bid up the price.

Here are some collectibles people were buying in 1980 and the average annual rate at which they have been increasing in value over the last 10 years:

- Chinese ceramics—18%
- Rare books—16.5%
- Gold—16.3%
- Stamps—15.4%
- Coins—13%
- Diamonds—12.6%
- Paintings (old masters)—11.6%

Gold went through a period of extraordinary rapid growth in value during 1979. This was caused partly by the fact that foreigners—mainly Arabs, Germans, and Japanese—held great quantities of American paper dollars and were losing confidence in them. So they used them to buy gold. But this is an unusual situation, and the rate of growth should return to the 10-year average rate when those groups have divested themselves of some of their surplus dollars and discover that even gold fluctuates in price, based on supply and demand.

Contrast the growth of these collectibles with other kinds of investments, and you'll see why some people have made a study of these things and are investing in them. Here are some comparable increases in value per year during the past 10 years.

- Farm land—10.6%
- Housing—9.2% (much higher annual rate in some years)
- Consumer price index—6.1% (rising much faster now)
- Bonds—6.1%
- Stocks—2.9%

Although the average percentage increase in the price of housing over the past *ten* years has been 9.2%, in one area, the Twin Cities of Minneapolis and St. Paul, between 1978 and 1979 alone, the average sale price increased by 17.2% for single-family dwellings. For that particular year an investment in a home would have been one of the best ways to combat inflation, but over the long run, most experts doubt that this high rate of increase could be sustained. This is already borne out by the California experience where prices increased at enormous rates for two or three years, and then when they reached a place where most buyers couldn't afford to buy, the rate of increase dropped sharply.

So rather than try to hit the one unusual year for any collectible, it's better to plan your investments based on what you can afford to handle when you are ready to make a decision.

There are many other kinds of collectibles, ranging from autographs and letters from famous people to Christmas plates and antique cars. Most people will want to stay away from collectibles because they can lose their money unless they know something about them.

If you do want to look at them more carefully, here are some suggestions:

1. Deal only with reputable dealers and brokers.

2. Investigate carefully before committing money; get professional appraisals.

3. Put only a limited portion of your investment capital into "hard assets"—generally 20% is an absolute top.

4. Do not try to diversify too widely. Stick with one or two fields, and get as much knowledge about those as possible.

5. Invest for the long term. Many experts say 10 years is the minimum time before windfall gains can be realized, although that time is shortening.

6. Protect your investment by getting proper and adequate insurance; store small items in a bank vault, and keep careful records.

If you've never invested in collectibles, you might want to start out with something like plates. Collecting annual Christmas plates once was a hobby strictly for the purpose of enjoying the plates. They cost only $4 or $5 each and made nice decorations on the walls. However, in recent years, more and more people have become attracted to the hobby, and this has raised the price. As a result, more companies started to produce special-occasion plates, commemorating events as Mother's Day, Christmas, and Easter.

It's important to get some good advice before getting into collecting anything, even as low-priced as plates. But if you hit it right and have just a little knowledge along with the enjoyment of having the collection, you could find your investment increasing rapidly. But for the average person, investing in collectibles is probably not a good alternative.

WARRANTS

A warrant is a piece of paper that entitles the holder to buy shares of stock in the issuing company at a predetermined price, in most cases for a period of years. People usually buy warrants when they feel sure the company is going to do well and the price of its stock will rise.

Warrants enable buyers to get bigger returns for their investment, providing they are smart or lucky. If you happen to hit a rising market, your warrants guarantee you the right to buy stock at the lower price that existed at the time you purchased the warrant, for whatever the predetermined price might be. You can exercise that warrant at any time simply by selling it. What you get for it usually represents close to the current market-price of the stock, and for a fast-growing one, even more than the market price.

OIL INVESTMENTS

There are three types of investments you can make in oil partnerships. These are called exploratory partnerships, developmental partnerships, and income-producing partnerships. The first is the riskiest, but has the greatest potential for reward. The last is the least risky, but usually produces the lowest total return. Briefly, the differences are these:

1. **Exploratory partnerships.** This is an arrangement whereby you can purchase a limited partnership in an existing partnership through your stockbroker. The partnership company has secured exploratory rights for certain pieces of real estate. There's obviously a big risk involved, as they are strictly exploring and may or may not hit oil.

    To invest in this kind of speculative investment, you should be in a 60% to 70% tax bracket, have a net worth of $250,000, and be interested primarily in tax shelter. You can write off up to 100% of your investment over 3 years, and up to 80% of it during the first year alone. But any income is straight taxable income when it is received. The write-off, though, is an excellent tax shelter. Most readers of this book will not have an interest in becoming a limited partner in an exploratory company.

2. **Developmental partnership.** This is a company that already has some oil wells in a piece of land, and is preparing to drill more. There is less risk as they already know there's oil in the area, but they may or may not bring in additional wells.

    To make this a useful investment alternative, you should be in at least a 40% tax bracket and have a net worth of at least $100,000. 70% to 90% of your investment can be written off as a business expense during the first two years after you have purchased it. Any income received from it is taxable as ordinary income, but the rapid write-off of the investment gives a good tax shelter.

3. **Income-producing partnership.** The general partner or lead partner goes out and buys producing wells from oil companies. This is because the oil companies make their money off the refining, wholesaling, transportation, and retailing steps. They don't make a large percentage of it from owning oil wells, so when they bring them in, they frequently sell them.

To make this kind of investment worthwhile, you should have an annual income of at least $20,000 per year and a $20,000 net worth. 10% to 30% of your investment can be written off as a tax-deductible expense over a period of normally three years. You can invest as little as $2500 originally to purchase a limited partnership in an income-producing partnership company.

The oil-producing partnership is a great inflation hedge. For example, as this is being written, the average price of oil produced in the U.S. is $16 a barrel, but the world price is $32 a barrel. In October of 1980, when the federal controls on the price of domestically produced oil were scheduled to be taken off, the price was likely to rise to near the world market price of $32. This additional income per barrel will keep you even with inflation for some time to come. As foreign producers continue to raise their price of oil, as they are likely to do, and domestic prices go up, you have a hedge against inflation which will rise continuously.

I am aware of only two companies that have income-producing partnerships. Your broker can advise you of the names of both of them, one of which has been operating for nearly 20 years, and one of which is much younger.

You are practically guaranteed a return on this last kind of investment. The general partner, the people running the company, must provide you an 8% net return after taxes before they can make anything. This is in their prospectus and contract. You should have it explained to you by your broker to make sure that you understand it thoroughly.

There are many other features from oil investments, including the automatic reinvestment in the oil partnership of all income, the fact you can have all income paid to you, or you can have it split with part of it reinvested or part of it paid to you.

Investing in oil partnerships scares most people because they think that great quantities of money are involved. However, as tax rates rise and the dollar value of incomes rise, more and more people are becoming interested in tax shelters as well as inflation hedges. These three kinds of limited partnerships, available to relatively small investors at the beginning level, are one possibility that should be looked into.

HIGHER-RISK INVESTMENTS

Getting into higher-risk investments, you can consider purchasing written options, commodity futures, speculative stocks, oil-drilling pools, and various kinds of tax shelters.

To give you an idea how risky some of these investments can be, 86% of those who buy options lose money. Only 14% make a profit. It's true that the 14% can make it big, but the risk is far too high for most people to take.

LOW-RISK INVESTMENTS

Various types of retirement plans and U.S. Savings bonds fall into the category of being low-risk investments. Many experts can give you details on them when you are at that stage of investment.

In Chapter 1 you were introduced to a woman who received a $3000 divorce settlement and wanted to know how to invest it. It was my recommendation that she purchase 90-day maturity government notes at her local Federal Reserve Bank or invest this money in money-market funds at her brokers. Each would have given her an interest rate of around 12% and would at least let her stay close to inflation.

Also in Chapter 1 you met Terri Bates, who had $9000 in savings certificates. Since she was earning sufficient money to pay all of her living expenses and had no desire to purchase any real estate, she eventually invested in a good contract for deed. As an alternative, she could have set up $5000 of her $9000 in short-term U.S. government notes or in a money-market fund drawing approximately 12% at the then current rates. The remaining $4000 she could have split and put half into two and three blue-chip, high-quality, high-dividend stocks, such as the high-grade utility (power-and-light) stocks. She would then have enrolled in the automatic dividend reinvestment plan, and each quarter she would have added a little to the investment in these three good dividend stocks. The remaining $2000 could have been used to buy a corporate bond, yielding about 12%, from which she would have received periodic checks. The $2000 bond is her "hedge" against deflation. If interest rates drop, as they someday will, her bond will increase in value.

The $5000 would be available on short notice to cover any emergencies that might arise; the remaining $2000 would be earning a good interest return (through dividends), based on current purchase prices and interest rates, and also have a chance of appreciating in value as these corporations continue to grow, which most will.

Another alternative place for Terri would have been to put $5000 into the previously mentioned U.S. notes or money-market funds, in order to keep that much immediately available. She might be able to find a contract for deed or second mortgage small enough to purchase with the remaining $4000. If that C/D is discounted 20%, it would have a face or maturity value of $5000. If the interest rate on the original $5000 was 10%, she would be receiving $500 per year in interest (12% on the $4000 invested) plus a small amount on the principal. By putting the interest and principal monthly payments into her money-market fund and then using the final principal payment when the balloon payment becomes due, preferably in not more than three years, she could then remove everything over $5000 from the money-market fund and use it to buy an even larger, but still heavily discounted, contract for deed.

There's a little more risk and a little more administration involved in buying a C/D than investing her money in blue-chip common stocks or the various savings instruments, but there is also a chance to get a yield on her money of 18% or more; whereas the common stocks may or may not grow enough to give her that much total yield during the same period of time.

Remember, there is nothing wrong with wanting to increase your yield, but there is always the danger that you may become entangled in your investments. Also, remember that successful investments may lead to increased temptations. "But those who want to get rich fall into temptation and are caught in the trap of many foolish and harmful desires, which put them down to ruin and destruction. For the love of money is a source of all kinds of evil. Some have been so eager to have it that they have wandered away from the faith and have broken their hearts with many sorrows" (1 Tim. 6:9-10).

But God does not want us to be paupers. He wants us to handle the money he gives us wisely. Jesus said, "Well, then, you should have deposited my money in the bank, and I would have received it all back with interest when I returned. Now, take the money away from him and give it to the one who has ten thousand coins. For to every person who has something, even more will be given, and he will have more than enough; but the person who has nothing, even the little that he has will be taken away from him" (Matt. 25:27-29).

12

Adjusting
Your Priorities

Teach us to number our days and recognize how few they are. Help us to spend them as we should (Psalms 90:12).

One of the secrets of happiness and satisfaction in life, and at the same time of financial contentment, is to establish a personal hierarchy of values. How much of our lives do we spend chasing after things which are not very important to us? When we finally reach some of these goals, we find that our victories are hollow and that they really didn't bring much happiness after all.

The same is true of spending money for things we think we "just have to have," but which, when we acquire them, don't turn out to be very important.

Several years ago I did an exercise that opened my eyes to what I had almost unconsciously established as priorities in my own life. After listing all of the activities I was involved in, all the things I had accumulated, and the amount I was spending on each, I discovered that much of my time and money was going toward things that weren't really important to me. I also discovered that many things that were truly dear to me were getting very little of my time, attention, and money. Doing this exercise may be the most important part of this book for you.

At the end of this chapter you will find a form called "A Look in the Mirror." On it you can establish your own hierarchy of personal values. Follow the instructions below.

First, in the column under *Our Possessions,* list all of the things that you own that you might lose, or that might be taken away from you. This would include your health, your family, your church, your Christian faith, your job, your house, your lake cabin, your automobile, your friends, and everything else that you live with, depend on, and enjoy.

In the second column, under the heading *Our Time,* list the estimated percentage of your time that you give to each of these things every year. Make this the direct application of time. For example, if you say that you are working 12 hours every day, but are doing it for your family, you are probably kidding yourself. Your family could likely get along with less of the money you are earning, but would undoubtedly cherish more of your time. Consequently that 50% of your time is going to your job, not to your family, and should be listed after *job.*

If you are spending only 30 minutes per day with your family, talking with them, playing with them, and doing things together with them, then the percent of your time with your family would be only 1/48th of your time, or 2.08%. Make similar allocations of your time, and make them honestly, to every one of your "possessions."

In the third column, under *Our Money,* list the amount of money you spend on each of your "possessions."

If you are spending a considerable amount on a new car through monthly payments and upkeep, put it under the possession of *Car.* Don't deceive yourself by putting it under the possession of *Job* or *Family,* as neither one needs the new car. Both could get along with a less expensive car.

If you are giving 10% of the money that God has entrusted to you back to him through your church, you would list that 10% after *Church.* (Incidentally, you should also be giving at least 10% of your *time* to the work of your church, whether it be singing in the choir, teaching a Sunday school class, or putting in a good word for the Lord at your place of employment.)

The real payoff comes in the fourth column. Rate each of your possessions in their order of importance to you. What would be the first possession that you would give up? That would be the one that is least important to you. What would you give up second, third, and so on until you are down to your last five? In that list of five you will probably have God, your family, your job, your church, and one other that might vary greatly.

As you know, thousands of people throughout the centuries have been given the choice of giving up their faith —giving up their allegiance to God—or giving up their lives. Many have chosen to lose their lives rather than their God and faith. When we are asked what is of greatest importance to us, it forces us to decide where our priorities lie.

If you are like I was the first time I did this exercise— and it took me a long time to do it—you may discover you are spending much of your time and money on things that are of little importance to you.

Why not rearrange your personal hierarchy of values? Why not start spending more of your time and money on things which are of greatest value to you? Why not be like Job, who, when he lost everything, including his family and even his health, held tightly to his faith in God? When stripped of all the tinsel and temporary luxuries and temptations of this world, Job was free to examine his faith and his Creator. Through his faith, which was his top priority, he learned once again what Christ would say many centuries later, "But seek first his kingdom [God's] and his righteousness, and all these things shall be yours as well" (Matt. 6:33 RSV).

Recently I visited the Middle East and saw some of the better-known sites where men's lives were sorely tempted by a desire for things of this world.

First, I climbed Mount Sinai and sat at the top reading Exodus 20–32, reflecting on the great gifts that God gave there through Moses.

Forty days after Moses climbed that mountain to get the Ten Commandments and other laws, he returned to the Israelites, who were camped at the foot of the mountain. During his absence they had melted down their golden earrings and made a golden calf. They had to have a god whom they could see and touch in order to feel secure. They wanted something that was shiny and new and had what they felt was great value in this world.

Although we are often quick to criticize those Hebrews for wanting something physical to worship, how soon do we forget our worship of a new house, a new car, or even a new suit of clothes or dress.

I went from there to the Mount of Temptation and climbed to a tiny monastery, clinging to the side of the cliff. It was to the top of this barren mountain that Christ came after being baptized in the River Jordan.

In this wilderness Jesus went through the same kinds of temptation that all of us go through, only multiplied manyfold. Three times he was tempted by the devil with physical and material things of this world.

After Jesus spent 40 days and 40 nights fasting, Satan tempted him by telling him to turn the nearby rocks into bread. When we are hungry and weak, we are most susceptible to the temptations of this world. The same holds true when our physical senses are dulled, such as by emotional stress, drugs, or alcohol. At those times particularly, temptations result in our deciding to do things that we normally would not do, one of which is to spend money we don't have.

Second, he was taken to the top of the wall of the temple in Jerusalem, the Eternal and Holy City, and told to hurl himself down. Then if his heavenly Father were real, he would be caught and saved. But Jesus said, "You shall not tempt the Lord your God." Yet some of us today tempt God frequently, and challenge him daily to produce physical things for us.

Finally the devil showed Jesus all the kingdoms of the world and said they would all be his if Jesus would only bow down to him. I can just hear some politician saying, "You can't do any good for anybody until you get elected to office, so anything goes during the campaign!"

The third mountain I climbed was Mount Tabor, the most widely accepted site of the Transfiguration, where Christ spoke with Moses and Elijah and where his appearance was changed.

Jesus took Peter, James, and John, three of his closest followers, with him to the top of the Mount of Transfiguration. But while witnessing one of the greatest spiritual events of all time, Peter could not divorce himself from the things of this world. His response was, "If you wish, I will make three tents here, one for you, one for Moses, and one for Elijah" (Matt. 17:4). How typical it is of those of us who have our priorities confused. Even Peter, who walked with Jesus daily, could not separate the important from the irrelevant.

The real secret of financial success and security is to put God first in our lives. Once you have established your own list of priorities, you will learn to be satisfied with those things that you have finally discovered are most important to you. The acquisition of all of those lower priority things that cost money, and the clamoring for them which spends your energy, health, and enthusiasm for life, will be a thing of the past.

You will then be satisfied. The Bible says, "Keep your lives free from the love of money, and be satisfied with what you have, for God has said, 'I will never leave you; I will never abandon you' " (Heb. 13:5).

A LOOK IN THE MIRROR

Our Possessions	Our Time	Our Money	Importance Rating
1.	1.	1.	1.
2.	2.	2.	2.
3.	3.	3.	3.
4.	4.	4.	4.
5.	5.	5.	5.
6.	6.	6.	6.
7.	7.	7.	7.
8.	8.	8.	8.
9.	9.	9.	9.
10.	10.	10.	10.
11.	11.	11.	11.
12.	12.	12.	12.
13.	13.	13.	13.
14.	14.	14.	14.
15.	15.	15.	15.

13

Changing
Your Life-style

*Be concerned above everything
else with the Kingdom of God
and with what he requires of you,
and he will provide you with all
these other things (Matt. 6:33).*

Faced with the choice of changing our minds, or defending a previously held position, even though we know
it is weak, we will usually elect to defend our position.
The same thing applies to our life-style.

Faced with the choice of changing our life-style or fig-
uring out ways to continue it, we will frequently do
everything possible to continue living as we always have.
In times of inflation almost everyone is faced with this
choice.

The first thing most people think about is ways in
which they can get the additional money needed to maintain their present life-style. If only the husband is working, the first move is to put the wife to work. This will
usually bring in some additional income, but there is a
price to pay. Part of that price is having the wife out of
the home during the day. If the couple has no children,
few problems arise. But if there are children, new expenses

and possible new problems with the children are often the result.

New expenses include day care for the children, new clothing for the working mother, additional transportation expenses including possibly a second car, and even expenses for the little things, such as lunches, cosmetics, beauty parlor bills, and more dinners out. The biggest price may be the one paid by the children who are dropped off at a neighbor's house to wait for the school bus each morning and return home to an empty house each afternoon. The price in human terms may far exceed the value of maintaining the old life-style.

A far better approach is simply to reduce the amount we are spending to live. It's much more desirable to change our style of living than it is to take a wife and mother out of the home in order to maintain an overly materialistic style of living. But we resist change, regardless of the cause.

If we have always driven our car to work, starting when gasoline was 29.9¢ per gallon, we'll resist changing our way of getting to the office even though gas now costs four times that amount. We'll spend less for food, clothing, recreation, and probably give less to the church, but we'll keep right on buying just as much gasoline, as long as it's humanly possible.

Similarly, if it has been our habit to eat out with the boys every noon, we'll keep right on doing it, even though that lunch now costs $4.50 rather than the $1.50 of only a few years ago. Our salaries have not tripled, though the cost of the meal has. But it's our life-style to have that good 90-minute lunch hour every day with the boys. Faced with the choice of changing that part of our routine, or cutting someplace else, we'll keep on having that expensive daily lunch.

Then there are the regular Saturday and Sunday golf

games. We've been playing together for years, and despite the fact that greens fees have gone from $4 to $12, we will not change. It's part of our life-style to have those two games every weekend, and we would never consider playing after four o'clock in the afternoon when the rates are cut in half or skip a week now and then. Again, faced with a change in our life-style or scrambling to keep it what it was, we'll elect the latter.

Every year our family has taken its two-week vacation at a resort up in the wilderness area of our state. It's been the same resort every year, the same two weeks every year, and we've thoroughly enjoyed it every year. The costs have been rising 10% per year, not counting the gasoline. Our incomes have been creeping up only about 5% per year, but it is our life-style to have that two-week vacation and, come what may, we'll find a way to do it, even if we have to get a vacation loan from the bank.

A time of inflation is a good time to reevaluate all that we are doing and to establish some new life patterns and perhaps a whole life-style.

CARS

You don't have to drive to work by yourself five days a week. You can discipline yourself to enter a car pool and arrive at the office the same time as the other three or four people in that car pool. You can also plan your work so that it's finished by the time the rest of them are ready to go home. If you can't get it done, either you aren't using your time wisely, or the job is too big for you to handle. On the theory that your supervisor knows what he is doing when he assigns you the work, it's more likely the former. A little less time at the water cooler, at coffee breaks, and at those fancy luncheons will have you ready to go home when the car pool leaves.

How nice it will be for you to have to drive only once each week, rather than the old five times. And how nice it will be to avoid those high-priced fill-ups and that gas line if a shortage hits.

You can change your transportation life-style in many other ways. Some people are already changing from big gas-guzzling cars to smaller ones. Others have stopped buying new cars and are buying only used cars and discovering they run just as well.

Still other families have cut down from three cars to two or two cars to one, and discovered that somehow they manage to get along just fine. Some are even thinking back to that time only a generation ago when most families had no cars and managed to live happily. And many others have discovered the buses and trains are still running.

HOUSING

Changing our housing life-style can be even more difficult and traumatic. Just as we drive "gas guzzlers," some of us really live as "space guzzlers." Most of us occupy houses which are far bigger than we need. It's tough to admit it, but there are many single people and childless couples occupying three-bedroom homes with full basements and huge living rooms, dining rooms, kitchens, and frequently two baths. It's pretty hard to justify using that much space and the gas and oil it takes to heat it, the electricity it takes to light it, plus all of the other upkeep.

These situations, in which we occupy more space than we need and cause more work and anxiety for ourselves trying to pay for it and keep it up, usually sneak up on us. At one time the house was full of kids, but as they grew up and moved away, we needed less and less space. We hold onto it because the kids might come and visit some day. Then when one of the partners in the marriage dies, the situation seems to continue. The house has many memories, we have many sentimental attachments to it, and it's hard to balance these off against a waste of living space and the high cost of upkeep.

The growth of condominiums has been particularly helpful in getting people to switch from big-home ownership to a different kind of property ownership. They still have their security, but it's in fewer square feet.

My mother's downward progression in living space has been an example. When all six children were home, we lived in a four-bedroom house. Mother and dad stayed on in that house as one by one we married and moved away. Then when dad died, mother moved into a duplex. It had one-fourth the space of the house, still far more than she needed. But she was comfortable and could afford it.

As her physical condition deteriorated, she didn't want to take care of a three-bedroom duplex any longer, so she moved into a one-bedroom apartment. That was a nice arrangement and gave her enough space until further deterioration of her health made it difficult for her to prepare her own meals and get around.

By then she was ready to move into a retirement home where her private living space shrank to one 8' x 12' room. Along the way she shed much of her furniture and other possessions which at one time she felt she couldn't get along without. She quickly forgot about most of them. In the retirement home she has access to the public lounges, but seldom uses them. She also has access to the dining room, which she uses three times each day. But she's perfectly content and comfortable in that small single room with only four or five pieces of her original house full of furniture.

Perhaps it's the psychological adjustment that's more

important than the physical adjustment, but whatever it is, it's time for many people to change their housing life-style before they are forced to do so financially. We simply occupy much more space than we need, and at a time when every square foot of floor space is expensive, unless you are paying well below the market rate for the space you are occupying, if finances are tight, it's time to move.

EATING OUT

What about those five weekly luncheons out? Perhaps the other men who have been a part of this ritual are in the same situation as you. They might just be waiting for someone to break the ice by saying, "Why don't we carry our lunches and eat in the office four days every week? In that way, we'll have more time to visit and, perhaps, even have a fast card game during our lunch break. Then when we do go out for lunch on Friday, we can make it a real celebration."

It's a break in a long-established pattern and a change in life-style, but it will save you money. You'll also have your day's work finished in time to make the car pool trip home.

VACATIONS

What about those annual two-week vacations at that favorite family resort? Everyone needs a vacation, and it wasn't too many years ago that dad would pack the family into the car and take off for a trip to Yellowstone, Glacier National Park, Lake Louise, the beach, or one of hundreds of other stops along the way.

Families once thought nothing of loading the children

into their recreational vehicle, which got six miles to the gallon, hooking a motorboat on the back, and setting off for the Northwoods on a Friday afternoon. They would return late Sunday after burning up 60 or 70 gallons of gasoline, another 15 gallons in the boat towing water skiers, and the equivalent amount for food and beverages.

On the way north, they probably passed a hundred equally beautiful spots, and on the way back, after an exhausting weekend, probably asked themselves why they had gone so far and driven so much to enjoy only a few hours.

American vacation habits are changing, and the combination of inflationary costs and energy shortages are doing it. With the cost of "recreation and education" running between 4% and 10%, it is a key item in your family budget. Resorts near population centers, movie theaters, and bowling alleys are all prospering again as more people avoid the far-away vacation spots. Others are rediscovering the joys of neighborhood activities— swimming, tennis, cycling, barbeques — and buying the necessary equipment (frequently second-hand) to enjoy them.

It's a paradox that people are staying home to save money, but spending record amounts for backyard swimming pools, new bicycles, and all the other gear and equipment they think they need to enjoy themselves at home. Others, however, are making use of public beaches in record numbers and have rediscovered the joy of simply sitting in their backyards, on their front porches, or at the neighborhood park.

Most cities also provide a wide variety of year-round entertainment. We are rediscovering our own art galleries, small playhouses, amateur shows, the joys of jogging, and the fun of fishing in a local stream or lake.

Neighborhood bowling alleys in 1980 were reporting a 25% increase in receipts over a year earlier when gasoline was plentiful, and the cost of rolling two or three lines is far below the cost of driving 200 miles to catch a few panfish.

Even pay television is booming as people watch more TV to enjoy their leisure time. They have apparently tired of the reruns, the incessant advertising, and are not intrigued by some of the ongoing serials. So they look to cable television for first-run movies and other entertainment which, without frequent interruption for commercials, is more enjoyable.

Then there is always the public library and reading. When more money was available, it was easier to purchase the latest bestseller. But hardback editions of books now may cost from $10 to $15, and many have discovered them in their local library. If the library does not have the book it may buy it if you request it.

Touring the state capital or city hall, or taking a free tour of a local manufacturing plant, automobile assembly plant, utility company, or other businesses is a fascinating way to spend a half-day or more of your vacation. Combine it with a picnic dinner, and your family will have a day that will be far more enjoyable than getting up at the crack of dawn to drive 600 miles before plopping exhausted into a sagging motel bed.

Perhaps we're spending too much money on vacations. A little more ingenuity in planning them will give us more satisfaction and less cost.

RECREATION

During the balance of the year, why not give a little thought to giving up at least one of those two weekend golf games? Play your Saturday morning game like you've always done, but skip the Sunday game and go to church with your family. You, your family, and God will be glad you've changed that part of your life-style.

You may even want to go out late Sunday afternoon, when the greens fees are cut in half, but with your family. Perhaps one of your children or your wife would like to take up your favorite recreation. It may be a little difficult for you the first few times, but soon you'll become more interested in their improving their game than in improving your own. When you reach that point, you'll have changed your life-style again, and your family will love you even more for it.

Many other forms of recreation have made comebacks in recent years, for example, taking a walk. That had become an out-of-style activity for a long time. Driving your car to a movie or to a high-priced athletic event was much more popular. Now a walk through the neighborhood or a park is gaining popularity and is much more healthy.

Riding bicycles has gained steadily as a recreational activity. It has become standard transportation for some, as it has been in Holland, Denmark, and other parts of the world for a long time.

Why not list all the recreational activities available within walking distance of your home. You'll be amazed at how little it costs to enjoy yourself.

As inflation forces you to consider new life-styles, remember that all spending is to be done to the glory of God. Paul wrote, "Whatever you do, whether you eat or drink, do it all for God's glory" (1 Cor. 10:31).

As we know from God's asking his disciples to gather up the scraps left over from feeding the 5000, he doesn't want anything to be wasted. But often we waste much in an effort to maintain a life-style which no longer fits, nor satisfies, nor meets our financial limitations. As we are faced with the choice of defending our old positions or changing them, let's be mature enough to drop the defenses and pick up the changes. Our lives will be richer for it. "And with all his abundant wealth through Christ Jesus, my God will supply all your needs" (Phil. 4:19).

14

Planning
for a Depression

And Jesus went on to say, "And so I tell you: Make friends for yourselves with worldly wealth, so that when it gives out, you will be welcomed in the eternal home. Whoever is faithful in small matters will be faithful in large ones; whoever is dishonest in handling worldly wealth, how can you be trusted with true wealth? And if you have not been faithful with what belongs to someone else, who will give you what belongs to you?" (Luke 16:9-12).

Most people, it seems, are so busy trying to handle inflation by buying unneeded things before the prices go up that they have forgotten there might also be a depression just around the corner.

Consequently there's always risk involved when you buy something if you have to borrow money to pay for it. There's also risk involved if you buy something by using all your savings, and a bigger risk if you have no savings at all.

In a time of depression, or a smaller depression called a recession, money normally becomes more valuable than things. This is because people can't eat things, and they need money to buy food. So they start to sell their things. Better buys appear for automobiles, particularly used cars. Good buys appear on used furniture market because people who are overextended have to convert some of their things to cash in order to meet everyday expenses.

Even the retailers of such items as new furniture, new cars, and new clothing have to get cash to pay their bills. Most of them accept cars and merchandise without actually paying for it. Sometimes they buy their merchandise on credit granted by the manufacturers or wholesalers, and other times they carry their inventory by borrowing from banks. Either way, unsold merchandise means they have to pay interest much longer. They are always anxious to sell the merchandise, pay off the loans, and cut that interest drain on their cash.

In times of depression good buys are available from those who sell things new, and even better buys are available from those who sell things secondhand.

Most important of all, even if you're not going to buy anything except food and shelter, you should have some way to do it. Here are some ways you can plan for a depression.

1. In good times do not commit your full income to living expenses (including debt payments). You must have a cushion to fall back on. This is why we strongly urge everyone to take the second 10% (first is your tithe) off the top of his or her income and put it into some sort of safe, secure, yet liquid savings. In good times this helps you build up a nest egg that can be put to work earning

more income for you. If a depression comes along, it is the cushion that permits you to continue to make house payments and feed and clothe your family until economic conditions improve.

If, however, you spend every penny you make during good times, you'll never accumulate that reserve to work for you, and you'll never have the cushion you need to tide you over the down cycles. "Sensible people will see trouble coming and avoid it, but an unthinking person will walk right into it and regret it later" (Prov. 22:3).

2. In good times, pay cash for everything you buy except your home or income-producing real estate. The only exceptions are routine and recurring cost of living items, such as 30-day charges at department stores, utilities, and gasoline. As long as you are able to pay these at the end of each month, you may continue to charge them.

Think of the mess you'd be in if you lose your job and have monthly payments to make for your car, television set, washing machine, bedroom set, and that beautiful new boat and motor. Without savings, there'll be no cash to do it, and the down payment you have put into each will be lost when it is repossessed.

3. Avoid long-term commitments requiring two salaries, or one salary plus overtime. In a time of depression when people are laid off, it may be that either you or your spouse will lose your jobs. If your house payments and other irreducible commitments are based on two salaries, you'll end up by losing something.

Sometimes it's permissible to take the risk of buying a house when monthly payments can be met only by taking money out of the salaries of each spouse. Even then try to save 10% from each salary every month. If a recession does come and one of you gets laid off, you'll have that reserve to help make those house payments until that spouse can find at least part-time or temporary employment.

If you plan your expenditures to use up both your salaries completely, plus overtime and production bonuses, you're in trouble. Pull those expenses back down to the place where your overtime and bonuses are not committed. That's a vital first step. It will help you prepare to meet the day when and if a recession comes. Then pull back 10% further and start setting up that savings safety valve.

4. Try, in good times, to determine how depression-proof your job is. Some jobs are stable almost regardless of the economy's condition. The telephone companies, electric utilities, many types of government work, and others are secure regardless of inflation or depression. Other types of jobs are sensitive to any downturn. Assembling automobiles might be one example. If you're in such a sensitive industry or have an easily dispensable job, get into something more stable while times are good, even though the starting pay might be lower.

5. Understand your backup sources of income, if any, before you are laid off. Unemployment compensation, union benefits, and salary continuation plans might be available. How much and how long would these benefits finance your needs?

6. Explore ways your present assets can be put to work for you. When a homeowner starts planning for a depression, particularly when it follows a long inflationary period, he or she has an excellent new way of riding out that period of economic problems. He can get monthly payments from a bank or savings-and-loan association, in states where the law permits, and use their equity in their house for security. Here's how it works:

If you have lived in your house for a long time, you probably have paid the mortgage down or might have paid it off altogether. Even if you have purchased your house within the last few years, if it was during an inflationary period, the market value is probably much higher than your purchase price. We don't really know whether or not the prices of houses are going to drop significantly during any future recession, but most economists think because the cost of building new houses will probably change little, and the purchasing power of the dollar has been permanently damaged, that house prices will drop relatively little. Consequently, even though you might have purchased your home only four or five years ago, inflation alone has probably given you a big increase in your equity.

To get long-range income needed to pay your living expenses or to tide you over a difficult period, you can apply for what is called reverse annuity mortgage. These mortgages, which are available in some states, provide that the bank or savings and loan will send you an agreed-on amount of money each month (say $250) for a period of time that you agree on (perhaps five years). At the end of that period, you will probably sell your home in order to repay the loan. If you have previously determined that you will want to live in your home only five more years, or some such period, it could be a good arrangement for you. If, however, you want to live in your home much longer than that, you will find yourself faced with repaying that mortgage, which might not be such a good deal.

This is probably a good protection against depression or economic hard times mainly for older people. In the United States 70% of the elderly live in their own homes, and 84% of these own their own homes free and clear. Many of them would like to live in their homes for just a few more years, but find it difficult to do so on their relatively fixed incomes. This type of loan could be a good thing for them. At least it's another plan for a depression that you can tuck away in the back of your mind and explore thoroughly when the time comes.

7. Prepare yourself to handle different types of work. If you are working on an assembly line, you should be learning new skills such as typing, printing, or bookkeeping. These can be learned at area vocational/technical schools in night classes, and will give you a much better opportunity of finding a new job if you are laid off.

8. Do not put yourself in the position of carrying someone else's debts. If a friend has trouble getting a loan and asks you to cosign for him, it's natural to want to help. But what you are really doing is helping him to get into debt over his head. Furthermore, over 50% of cosigners are called on to pay off these loans. You may hurt your friend by trying to help him, and likely will hurt your family by adding to your financial burdens. That's why the Bible says, "Only a man with no sense would promise to be responsible for someone else's debts" (Prov. 17:18).

9. Understand and list any other sources of help that might be yours. For example, you can probably skip premium payments on certain life-insurance policies, pension plans, and maybe even the principal part of your home payments. But know what these options are before you are forced to use them.

10. If you don't have a written budget now, set one up immediately (see Chapter 8). Whenever you are setting up a budget, always visualize the worst thing that could happen to your income. If you do, you'll plan and live conservatively, and a disaster which you cannot handle will never occur.

During a period of recession in our economy, or a personal recession, when you are without a job or other income, you can fall back on your savings. The length of time your savings will last depends upon how much you have saved, how much you draw out at the end of each month, and the interest rate it is earning. The following chart shows how long your savings could last. Both interest earned and percent withdrawn are figured on a yearly basis, then divided into 12 monthly installments.

Percent of savings withdrawn

Interest rate paid	5%		6%		7%		8%		9%		10%	
	yrs.	mos.	yrs.	mos.	yrs.	mos.	yrs.	mos.	yrs.	mos.	yrs.	mos.
5%	oo		37	0	25	6	19	11	16	5	14	0
6%			oo		33	8	23	7	18	7	15	6
7%					oo		31	1	22	1	17	6
8%							oo		28	11	20	9
9%									oo		27	2
10%											oo	

Percent of savings withdrawn

Interest rate paid	11%		12%		13%		14%		15%	
	yrs.	mos.	yrs.	mos.	yrs.	mos.	yrs.	mos.	yrs.	mos.
5%	12	3	10	10	9	9	8	11	8	2
6%	13	3	11	8	10	5	9	5	8	7
7%	14	8	12	6	11	2	10	0	9	1
8%	16	7	14	0	12	2	10	9	9	8
9%	19	7	15	9	13	4	11	8	10	4
10%	25	7	18	7	15	1	12	10	11	2
11%	oo		24	4	17	9	14	5	12	4
12%			oo		23	2	17	0	13	11
13%					oo		22	3	16	4
14%							oo		21	4
15%									oo	

oo infinity

To use this chart find out what the interest rate is on your savings; then determine what percentage of your savings you want to withdraw. Using this chart, you can see that if each month you withdraw 6% of your savings,

and have the remainder invested at 5%, you could continue withdrawing 6% per month for a total of 37 years.
It would last this long because the balance of your savings account continues to earn 5% (compounded continuously under a formula called 365/360), so that most of
what you are withdrawing is being regenerated by the
interest.

Looking across the chart, you can see that if you withdraw 10% of your savings each month and have it invested at an interest rate of only 5%, your money will
be gone in "only" 14 years.

When you plan for defensive moves that you might be
forced to make during an extended job layoff or other
loss of income, it is wise to figure out how long your current savings will last if you withdraw a specific percentage
every month. This will not only give you a greater sense
of security, but will also give you another incentive to tuck
away that 10% each pay day and put it into an interest-
earning savings account.

15

That Elusive
Ten Percent

Remember that the person who plants few seeds will have a small crop; the one who plants many seeds will have a large crop. Each one should give, then, as he had decided, not with regret or out of a sense of duty; for God loves the one who gives gladly. And God is able to give you more than you need for yourselves and more than enough for every good cause (2 Cor. 9:6-8).

Throughout this book it has been suggested that you take 10 percent off the top of your income and give it to the work of the Lord. What you are actually doing is returning to him 10 percent of all he has given you. Everything that we have belongs to him, and anything that we give to him, we really only return. "Do this so that you may learn to have reverence for the Lord your God always" (Deut. 14:23).

The purpose of tithing is not merely to raise money, although that is certainly needed to carry forward God's work in the world, but to teach us to put him first in our lives. This has many beneficial effects on everything we do. As it relates to finances, it means that the many things we normally would buy are no longer as important as they were and no longer will occupy the center of our lives. God is in that position, and we have learned to put him there through giving him the "first fruits" of all that we earn by giving a minimum of 10 percent.

With God at the center of our lives, most of our emotional problems also disappear. We're no longer worried about job security, the problems of others advancing over us or getting the best of us, and the emotional disturbances that arise from insecurities and fears. In addition to teaching us to put God first in our lives, tithing helps us melt away a wide range of problems.

The rich young man who came to Jesus asking what he must do to possess eternal life was told that he must keep the commandments. When he asked which ones, Jesus detailed them. Evidently not being satisfied with this answer, the man replied, "Ever since I was young, I have obeyed all these commandments."

Jesus answered, "There is still one more thing you need to do. Sell all you have and give the money to the poor, and you will have riches in heaven; then come and follow me" (Luke 18:21-22). When the young man heard this requirement, he departed in sorrow, for he was a man of great wealth.

Jesus was not interested in having the young man's money, even though he exhorted him to give it all away. What he wanted was to change the heart so the young man would trust not in his wealth but in God. The young man's money would continue to be at the center of his life until he no longer had it, and Christ knew this. If he had taken Jesus' advice, he would have been richer in ways he did not know. So it is with us. Whatever we give to the

Lord, including money, he will bless and return abundantly.

However, many people say, "I can't pay my bills as it is. How do you expect me to do so if I give the Lord ten percent off the top?" The Bible helps explain that through many of its teachings. One of them says, "Trust in the Lord with all your heart. Never rely on what you think you know. Remember the Lord in everything you do, and he will show you the right way" (Prov. 3:5-6).

People who tithe report an intangible "something" happens to their finances. They find they are not wasting money as they used to; they don't make bad financial decisions. As they walk in obedience to the Lord, they find "unheard-of" bargains that before had often turned out to be white elephants. One man told this story: "I wanted to buy a new car because the transmission was going out on my old one. I was severely tempted to stop tithing so I could make car payments. As soon as I made the decision to continue tithing, I discovered a mechanic who said the original analysis was wrong, and the car could be fixed for three dollars."

What more do we need than God's assurance to take him at his word and to trust him. Why don't you give it a try? You will be pleased with the results.

The Bible has many other instructions on how to go about giving our tithes and offerings to God, in order to put him first in our lives and also to further his work.

Some people measure their amount of giving by how much they can reduce their income taxes at the end of the year. So they give very little all year long, but if it looks as if they've had a good year and a sizeable gift to the church will be a badly needed tax deduction, then they will give. But this kind of giving misses the reasons for giving and, therefore, will miss the blessings from God. Such once-a-year giving is also a violation of Scripture.

Paul wrote, "Every Sunday each of you must put aside some money, in proportion to what he has earned, and save it up, so that there will be no need to collect money when I come" (1 Cor. 16:2).

If you give on a regular basis, you give because you are putting God first in your life. If you give once a year, you are doing so to take advantage of the tax laws. It's quite likely that God is not first in your life, and your gift means little to your way of living.

If you are still worried about whether or not you can make both ends meet if you return the top 10 percent of your income to him who has given you everything, you might want to reread Luke 6:38 which says, "Give to others, and God will give to you. Indeed, you will receive a full measure, a generous helping, poured into your hands —all that you can hold. The measure you use for others is the one that God will use for you." There's no way we can outgive God.

Remember, there is no better way to get your priorities in order than to "be concerned above everything else with the Kingdom of God and with what he requires of you, and he will provide you with all these other things" (Matt. 6:33).

It's a promise from God, our Lord and our Creator. Let's believe him, and do what he says. The rewards will start immediately and last for all eternity.

16

Making a Will

But all things should be done decently and in order (1 Cor. 14:40).

As is true with almost all other financial planning, the biblical admonition to look ahead, foresee difficulties, and prepare for them applies also to the distribution of your assets after your death.

A will is a written instrument by which you dispose of your property at your death. To be effective it must be written in compliance with each state's statutory provisions. And, as state laws vary from state to state, only your attorney can adequately advise you on the preparation of your will.

If you die without a written will, you are said to have died "intestate." Most people in this country die with no will, an invalid will, or an improperly drawn will. This means that the disposition of their assets no longer follows their wishes, but is handled in accordance with state law.

When you die, you are going to have a will one way or another. Either you write one, or your state government will have written one for you. And you might not be pleased with its provisions. "Nothing that I had worked for and earned meant a thing to me, because I knew that I would have to leave it to my successor, and he might be wise, or he might be foolish—who knows? Yet he will own everything I have worked for, everything my wisdom has earned for me in this world. It is all useless" (Eccles. 2:18-19).

Every will must pass through what is called probate court. Probate courts were established to ensure that the provisions of your will are carried out properly. There are ways to transfer some of your assets to members of your family, your church, and other people that may avoid the probate process. These include taking the necessary legal steps so your property is jointly owned with right to survivorship (joint tenancy). In this case on the death of any joint tenant, his or her share passes to the survivor or survivors. If all of the joint tenants die in an accident, this method of attempting to transfer property without going through the probate court and the will process has no effect. But as both or all joint tenants seldom die in a common disaster, this is a widely used and convenient way to transfer ownership of property.

Another type of joint ownership is called ("tenancy in common.") This property is held in such a manner that each owner has an undivided interest in the property. When one owner dies, ownership does (not) go to the other owner or owners (as in joint tenancy), but instead passes into the deceased person's estate.

There is yet another type of joint ownership. It is called (community property.) In 1980 eight states had community property laws: Arizona, California, Idaho, Louisiana, Nevada, New Mexico, Texas, and Washington. In these states each marriage partner automatically owns half of all property acquired during the marriage. So in the event of death, one-half of all property automatically belongs to the surviving partner of a marriage and does not have to be included in a will or go through probate.

PREPARING YOUR WILL

In preparing your will, consider the following, somewhat in this order:

1. It's a great place to give your final testimony to God, including a statement expressing your faith in him, your praise for him, and your gratitude to him in a natural and meaningful way.

2. Leave a minimum gift of 10% of all your net assets to the work of the Lord. You can do this through a direct bequest to your church, or you can divide that amount to your church and other Christian programs at home or abroad. But just as we give a minimum of 10% of our income to the work of the Lord while we are living, we should set aside this amount to keep on doing that work after we have died. "Every one of us, then, will have to give an account of himself to God" (Rom. 14:12).

3. For your younger children you should select guardians who would continue their Christian upbringing; you should also select guardians for your elderly parents or other relatives, if there are no other brothers or sisters to assume this Christian responsibility.

Before making such a selection and entering it into your will, you'll want to discuss it carefully with those whom you select and secure their agreement to it. In addition, it's wise to select a backup individual or couple in the event something happens to change the physical or economic circumstances of your first choice.

4. The fourth important decision is the naming of an executor. This is the person who will carry out your wishes and must be someone in whom you have complete faith and trust. The executor does not have to be a lawyer

or knowledgeable in laws relating to wills. He can get professional advice in those areas. But he does have to be someone you can trust, someone who will carry out your wishes as you have expressed them, and someone with the general good judgment to make sometimes difficult decisions.

COLLECTING INFORMATION

After these basic four considerations, here is the information you will need before you see an attorney or other qualified expert to assist you in the preparation of your will.

Personal Information

- Your name, in full, and date of birth
- Your address, both residence and business
- Your wife's maiden name and date of birth
- Your children and other dependents' names and ages

Estate Summary

- Market value of your home and amount of mortgage
- Approximate value of your personal effects (furniture, automobile, library)
- Market value of other real estate owned by you, and your investments (mutual funds, stocks, bonds, mortgages, savings accounts and certificates)
- The name of your business, if any, its approximate value, and whether it is a proprietorship, partnership, or corporation
- Amount of life insurance you carry (both group and personal), who owns the policies (you or your wife), and to whom they are payable
- How much cash you have in your checking account, and any other assets not listed above

- Your annual contribution to a pension plan and the present value of all your contributions
- Amount of money you owe to the bank or to others
- A record of how much money you earn each year

Disposition of Estate

- What do you want done with such items as your clothing, jewelry, personal effects, household goods, furniture, automobile?
- How do you want your residence disposed of? (to your spouse, or sold and the proceeds distributed to your heirs?)
- What provisions do you want to make for your wife and children? (For example, do you want her to have an income with power to encroach upon the capital for living purposes?)
- What provisions do you want for cash gifts or special bequests for churches, charitable institutions, or people?
- To whom would you like the residue of your estate to pass and at what age?
- What person or trust company would you like to handle your estate as sole executor or co-executor?
- Are there any special funeral instructions?
- If in business, what do you want done with it? (For example, do you want your spouse to carry it on if she or he is willing and able? Do you want someone else to keep it going? Or do you want it sold?)
- What is your desire for either broad or specific investment powers for your trustees and executors?
- What is the name and address of a guardian for your children in the event that both you and your spouse die before they are 21?
- What is the name and address of your accountant, if any?

Once you have prepared your notes as indicated above, you should telephone a lawyer in your area and make an appointment to see him. He will probably be surprised at the extent of your homework and will offer you the assistance you need to pull it all together into a functional will.

Do not put off having a will prepared. The fact that 36% of the American people die before they reach retirement age should be sufficient reason for you to act now.

Jesus once told this parable:

> There was once a rich man who had land which bore good crops. He began to think to himself, "I don't have a place to keep all my crops. What can I do? This is what I will do," he told himself; "I will tear down my barns and build bigger ones, where I will store the grain and all my other goods. Then I will say to myself, 'Lucky man! You have all the good things you need for many years. Take life easy, eat, drink, and enjoy yourself!' " But God said to him, "You fool! This very night you will have to give up your life; then who will get all these things you have kept for yourself?" (Luke 12:16-20).

TRUSTS

A trust is a written document placing ownership of your property in the name of one or more persons called *trustees,* to be held by the trustees for the use and benefit of some other person or persons. Several different types of trusts can be written. Some of those are:

1. *Testamentary.* A testamentary trust is created by you during your lifetime, but does not become active until after your death. It may be a separate document or part

of your will, but either way probatable assets must pass through your probate court before entering the trust.

(2.) *Living trusts, sometimes called "inter-vivos."* These are created by a living person and take effect during his lifetime. If properly written, the assets held in this type of trust will avoid probate. They can pass immediately to the beneficiary on the death of the writer of the trust.

Living trusts can be revocable or irrevocable. A revocable living trust is one that can be amended or terminated by the person who created it. As might be expected, an irrevocable living trust is one that cannot be changed or canceled. As a practical matter under current tax laws, testamentary or living trusts should be considered if an estate is $350,000 or greater.

(3.) Another interesting trust is called a *charitable remainder trust*. This is an arrangement with a charity under which you give them a gift, but they agree to pay the income earned by that gift to one or more persons for as long as those persons live. Then the gift becomes the property of the charity.

(4.) A similar type arrangement is commonly called a *clifford trust*. In this arrangement you place money or property with an independent trustee who is required to pay the income to another person for more than 10 years, or until the death of that other person, with the money or property then being returned to the person creating the trust, in this case you. It is frequently used as a way to give a gift to a college or university, or to help pay for a student's college education. This is one reason this kind of trust is frequently referred to as an "education trust."

Trusts are the most versatile and useful of all estate-planning devices, and if they are well drawn, estate taxes may be minimized. In addition, your specific directions are easily incorporated. Since a trust is a private document, it is not exposed to public scrutiny.

However, a trust does not take the place of a will. You must have a will in addition to the trust, and normally you would write the will first.

A trust can be set up by you for your own benefit, for the benefit of another individual, for the benefit of your family, or for the benefit of an educational, religious, or charitable institution.

When it is done, it will usually save taxes, provide for the specific disposition of all or part of your estate, and have many other legitimate benefits. As with every other one of these technical moves, look for a Christian counselor while you are able to do it.

At the time of death of any adult member of the family, necessary information must be secured immediately and should be readily available to the survivors. The form in Appendix A will assist you in providing a thoughtful record for your next of kin. They will deeply appreciate this service. File this with your personal papers. Attach it to your will. Review and revise it every few years.

Appendix A

Family Record

1. Date _____
2. Name _____
   Spouse _____
3. Address _____
   _____

4. Location of marriage certificate _____
   _____

5. Social Security or taxpayer's identification numbers:
   Husband _____ Wife _____
   Single _____
6. Date and place of birth
   Husband _____ Wife _____
   Single _____
7. Location of birth certificates _____
   _____

8. Names, addresses, and birthdates of children
   _____
   _____
   _____
   _____

9. Location of their birth certificates _____
   _____

10. Are there any deceased children? _____

11. If so, did they leave any children? Their names and birthdates.

_____

_____

12. If single, names and addresses of brothers, sisters, children of deceased brothers or sisters, parents, or other next of kin.

_____

_____

13. Location of documents proving the dissolution of any prior marriage by death or divorce _____

_____

14. Do you have a will? _____

15. Where is it kept? _____

16. Name and address of personal representative (executor) and attorney

_____

_____

17. If a veteran, where are your discharge papers?

_____

18. Are you entitled to veterans benefits? _____

19. Do you have disability rights? _____
    Military serial No. _____

20. Location of bank accounts and passbooks _____

_____

21. Are bank accounts joint and with whom? _____

_____

22. Location of safety deposit box and its key _____

_____

23. Is it joint and with whom? _____

_____

24. What real estate do you own and in what form is the ownership? (Sole ownership or joint tenancy?)

_____

_____

25. Location of deeds and property insurance ⎯⎯⎯⎯

26. Where is title insurance policy or deed or real-estate contract? ⎯⎯⎯⎯⎯⎯⎯⎯⎯⎯⎯⎯⎯⎯

27. Who holds the mortgage? ⎯⎯⎯⎯⎯⎯⎯⎯⎯⎯

28. What are the payments? ⎯⎯⎯⎯⎯⎯⎯⎯⎯⎯

29. Where is fire-insurance policy? ⎯⎯⎯⎯⎯⎯⎯⎯

30. What automobiles and boats do you own? ⎯⎯⎯⎯

31. Automobile-insurance company ⎯⎯⎯⎯⎯⎯⎯⎯

32. Are boats or autos subject to contract or mortgage?

33. What stocks, bonds, or mutual funds do you own? List the company, number of shares, purchase date, and price of each on back page.

34. Where are they kept? ⎯⎯⎯⎯⎯⎯⎯⎯⎯⎯⎯

35. List your life and health insurance policies, pensions or annuities, or interests in profit-sharing plans:

36. Who are the beneficiaries and where are the policies kept? ⎯⎯⎯⎯⎯⎯⎯⎯⎯⎯⎯⎯⎯⎯⎯

37. Do you have a cemetery lot? If so, where is the deed and what cemetery? ⎯⎯⎯⎯⎯⎯⎯⎯⎯⎯

38. If you have prearranged or prepaid funeral services, with what funeral home? ⎯⎯⎯⎯⎯⎯⎯⎯

39. List any instructions regarding funeral or burial (such as donation of organs, burial-society membership, beneficiary of memorial gifts in lieu of flowers).

_____

_____

_____

_____

40. List other valuable documents, such as promissory notes, contracts, pending patents, mutual-fund contracts, income-tax and gift-tax records, and where they are kept. _____

_____

_____

_____

_____

41. If you are engaged with anyone in any business venture or joint enterprise, list with whom and the details of the venture. _____

_____

_____

42. Do you have any debts or liabilities which could reduce your taxable estate? _____ Approximate amount _____

43 Further instructions _____

_____

_____

_____

_____

_____

_____

_____

_____

Appendix B

Glossary of Financial Terms

In this book we have used some terms which are not well known to many people, so most were explained briefly at the time they were used. However, we think it's important that more complete definitions be included. The following list contains most of the commonly used terms.

Acceleration clause: A provision allowing the lender to ask for full payment at once, if the loan installments are not paid when due.

Add-on charge: A method, no longer permissible, of advertising the interest rate on installment loans that understate the true interest rate.

Add-on clause: A provision allowing additional purchases on an exising installment credit agreement, normally stating that default in making payments on the additional purchases constitutes default on all purchases.

Administrator: One appointed to manage and distribute the estate of a deceased person who has not left a will, or where for some reason an executor has not been appointed or qualified under his will.

Affidavit: A statement sworn to or affirmed before an official who is authorized to administer oaths, usually a notary public.

After acquired property: Property which a debtor acquires after the execution of a mortgage or other form of indebtedness and which secures such indebtedness.

Amortize: Provision for repayment of a loan in periodic payments over a stated period of time.

Annual percentage rate (APR): Finance charge over a full year, expressed as a percentage, reflecting all costs of the loan as required by the Truth-in-Lending Act.

Appraisal: An estimate of value of property.

Appraisal fee: Charge for estimating the value of collateral being offered as security.

Asset: Something of value that can be used to repay debt.

Assignment: Transfer of an asset by one person known as the assignor to another known as the assignee. This action can be taken by either a creditor or a debtor to transfer an asset into the name of some third party.

Assignment of wages: In some states a debtor is permitted by law to give a creditor, or a collection agency, an assignment on his wage. This is a written statement to the effect that if the debtor defaults on his payment agreement, the assignment can be presented to the employer by the creditor or agency, and the employer is required to deduct a certain portion each pay period from the wages of the debtor and remit to the creditor or agency. Certain states specifically prohibit such wage assignments.

Attachment: A legal procedure by which the creditor requests the court to order the sheriff to seize property owned by the defendant and to hold and safeguard the same until such time as the court renders a decision in the matter.

Attorney-in-fact: A person who is authorized by power of attorney to act for another.

Balloon payment: Any payment which is more than twice

the amount of any other regularly scheduled equal payment.

Bank credit card: A credit card issued by a bank, enabling the borrower to buy goods and services or obtain a cash loan from banks honoring that card.

Bankruptcy: A court action declaring a person free of most debt, due to the inability of the person to pay.

Billing cycle: Time interval, often a month, between regular periodic billing statement dates.

Blank endorsement: Endorsement which consists only of the signature of the endorser and does not state in whose favor it is made.

Cash discount: Price reduction offered by merchants to customers paying in cash or by check instead of by credit card.

Caveat emptor: "Let the buyer beware" (Latin). In the absence of a warranty a buyer purchases goods at his own risk, unless the seller is guilty of fraud.

Charge account: Line of credit that may be used repeatedly up to a certain specified limit.

Chattel mortgage: A document offering property as security for payment of a debt.

Closing statement: An accounting of funds in a real-estate sale.

Collateral: Something of value pledged to assure loan repayment and subject to seizure upon default.

Collateral security: A separate obligation which is given to secure the performance of the primary obligation in a contract.

Co-maker or co-signer: A person, other than the borrower, who signs a note in order to give additional protection to the creditor granting the loan, because of the uncertain credit quality of the borrower.

Comparison shopping: Evaluation of a lender's annual percentage rate (APR), which tells the borrowers the relative cost of credit, against the APRs quoted by other lenders. Also applies to prices of merchandise.

Conditional sales contract: Document used in installment-sales credit-arrangements, which withholds ownership title from the buyer until the loan has been paid in full.

Consideration: The required element in all contracts by which a legal right or promise is exchanged for the act or promise of another person.

Consolidation loan: Combining several debts into one loan, usually to reduce the annual percentage rate or the dollar amount of payments made each month by extending them over a longer period of time.

Contract: Agreement between two or more parties. Certain legal formalities must be met.

Contract for deed: A legal instrument by which a borrower gives a creditor a lien on his property as security to a loan. It is usually used to secure a second loan on real estate that already carries a first mortgage.

Contractual liability: Obligation to repay all debts made in accordance with a contract.

Covenant: A promise by one person made to another.

Credit: An arrangement to receive cash, goods, or services now and pay for them in the future.

Credit application: A form filled out by a borrower wanting credit, or an interview, which seeks information about an applicant regarding residence, employment, income, and existing debt.

Credit bureau: A reporting agency which assembles credit and other information on consumers and supplies such information to others concerning a consumer's credit standing or capacity.

Credit history: A continuing record of a borrower's debt commitments and how well these have been honored.

Credit investigation: An inquiry undertaken by a lender

to verify information supplied by a borrower on a credit application.

Credit life insurance: Insurance covering the unpaid balance of a loan in the event of a borrower's death.

Creditor: A person or a business who regularly extends or arranges for the extension of consumer credit or lends money.

Credit rating: Evaluation of a person's previous credit experience.

Credit risk: The possibility of loss to a lender resulting from nonpayment by a borrower.

Credit-scoring system: A statistical measure used to rate credit applicants on the basis of various factors relevant to creditworthiness.

Current asset: An asset which may be converted into cash on short notice, such as stocks and bonds and savings deposits in a bank.

Debt collector: Anyone other than a creditor or his attorney who regularly collects debts for others.

Declining balance: The decreasing amount owed on a debt as monthly payments are made.

Default: Failure to perform that which is required by the terms of a credit agreement.

Defer: To delay payment to a future time.

Delinquent: A credit account which is past due and for which no satisfactory repayment arrangement has been made.

Disclosure: Information lenders must give to borrowers before a credit contract is signed.

Discount charge: Finance charge deducted in advance.

Discretionary income: What remains of disposable income after essential living costs are paid.

Disposable income: Take-home pay or net pay.

Down payment: A cash sum required at the outset of a

credit transaction, which together with the outstanding loan balance comprise the total cost.

Due date: A day of the month by which payment must be made.

Electronic fund transfer: Movement of funds initiated other than by check. Withdrawals or transfers at automated teller machines and debits to accounts at point of sale are EFTs.

Escrow: Funds to be paid by a second party to a third party on property held by the first party: for example, funds held by a bank—often collected together with monthly mortgage payments—to meet tax bills and insurance premiums.

Exemption: That portion of a debtor's property, either real or personal, or that portion of a debtor's wages or earnings, which cannot be attached, garnished or levied upon to satisfy a debt or judgment.

Extension: Agreement with the lender to allow the borrower, who may be having financial difficulties, to make smaller payments on an outstanding debt over a longer period of time.

Finance charge: Cost of a loan in dollars and cents as required by the Truth-in-Lending Act.

Foreclosure: A legal action by which the creditor exercises his legal rights to take possession of and sell mortgaged property. This procedure bars or extinguishes the debtor's right of redemption of the mortgaged property.

Garnishment: Court-sanctioned procedure by which a portion of a debtor's wages is set aside to repay creditors.

Grace period: A period of time after a due date not subject to late charges.

Gross income: Total earnings prior to deductions for taxes, health insurance, employee benefit plans, and other items.

Guarantor: One who agrees to pay the debt of another in the event the original maker of the obligation fails to pay. As a rule, such promises by a guarantor are not legally enforcible unless made in writing.

Holder in due course: Someone acquiring in good faith a purchaser's note. A legal doctrine previously separated the purchaser's obligation to pay the note from the seller's obligation to meet the terms of the sale.

Infancy: A person who has not attained the age at which he or she can enter into a legally binding contract. In some states, both men and women become of age when they are 21 years old, but in other states one or both become of age at 18. In law, all who are not "of age" are "infants."

Installment cash credit: A one-shot loan involving two parties: the borrower and the lender. The debt is repaid in equal installments over a specified period of time.

Installment sales credit: A one-shot loan used to buy items such as cars or appliances. A down payment is usually required, and a contract is signed for the balance due, plus interest and service charges. The debt is repaid in equal installments over a specified period of time. Generally involves three parties: the buyer, the seller, and the lender.

Instrument: A legal document, contract, note, or written agreement.

Investment: Anything acquired for the purpose of producing income or a profit.

Joint account: A credit arrangement for two or more persons, enabling all to use an account and assume liability to repay.

Land contract: Installment contract drawn between buyer and seller for the sale of property. Occasionally used as a substitute for a mortgage, except ownership of property does not pass until payment of the last installment.

Late charge: A percentage of the payment due which is charged for being late or paying after a predetermined grace period.

Legal action: Any proceeding in a court of law taken by a creditor in an effort to enforce collection of an account owned by a debtor.

Lessee: One who rents real or personal property from a lessor for a fee, called rent.

Liability: Legal responsibility to repay debt.

Lien: A claim which one person has upon property of another person, as security for debt; may also be created by law, as a mechanic's lien for unpaid bills due a home contractor.

Maker: The person who executes a promissory note or contract and has primary responsibility for payment.

Maturity date: Date on which final payment is due.

Mortgage: A legal instrument by which a borrower gives a creditor a lien on property as security for a loan; the lien created by the instrument.

Mortgage loan commitment: Written statement by lender to grant a specific loan amount, at a given rate, for a certain term, secured by a specific property, if the real-property transaction is closed before the expiration date.

Mortgagee: Lender of money on the security of a mortgage, that is, a bank.

Mortgagor: An owner of property who executes a mortgage covering property as security for a loan.

Net worth: Difference between total assets and total liabilities.

Note: A written document which is a recognized legal evidence of debt, promising payment of a specified sum of money on a certain date.

Open-account credit: Credit arrangement used by many retailers. Customers may purchase goods at any time up to a certain limit. Payment may be made for all purchases within 30 days with no interest charge applied, or in stated monthly payments based on the current account-balance, plus interest.

Open-end lease: Lease which may involve an additional payment based on the value of property when returned.

Overdraft checking: Line of credit permitting a person to write checks for more than the account balance, with interest charged on the amount borrowed.

Payment: Total sum of money borrowed, plus all finance charges, divided by the number of months in the terms of the loan.

Personal property: All rights and interest owned in goods or chattels or against another person, as distinguished from ownership of real estate.

Points: A loan discount, which is a one-time charge, used to adjust the yield on the loan to what market conditions demand. Each point equals one percent of the principal amount.

Principal: The actual amount of a loan before finance charges and other charges are added or deducted.

Probate: The act or process of providing a will or other instrument.

Real property: Land and everything that is permanently affixed to it.

Rebate: Portion of unearned interest returned to borrower if loan is repaid before the date designated for full payment.

Recording fee: Cost of recording necessary documents with the appropriate state or county administrative office.

Refinance: Revision of the payment schedule of existing debt.

Repossession: Act of reclaiming durable goods purchased on credit, for which payment is past due.

Rescission: Cancellation of a contract.

Reserve: Money or assets set aside, such as funds held by a lender to assure future payment for real-estate taxes or hazard insurance.

Revolving account: Line of credit that may be used repeatedly up to a certain specified limit.

Sales finance company: Lenders specializing in installment credit used to purchase durable items.

Satisfaction: Written evidence of the payment of a debt.

Secured note: A note containing a provision that on default certain pledged property may be claimed by the lender as payment of a debt.

Security: Assets which can be used to secure or guarantee payment of a financial obligation. Stocks, bonds, insurance, and real and personal property are considered excellent forms of security.

Security interest: An interest which a lender has in the borrower's property to assure repayment.

Service charge: Finance cost related to certain conditions of a credit contract, such as the fee when overdraft checking is activated.

Share draft: Check-like instrument enabling credit-union members to withdraw funds or pay bills from their credit-union share accounts.

Simple interest: A method of calculating interest on an outstanding balance that produces a declining finance charge with each payment of the installment loan.

Skip: Any debtor whose present whereabouts is not known.

Solvent: A good financial condition of an individual, firm, or corporation enabling them to pay their debts.

Statute of limitations: The time established by state law after which a debtor can no longer be forced, through legal proceedings, to pay an account. This period of time and the conditions under which this law applies differs from state to state.

Summons: A writ or notice requiring a person to appear before a court to answer a complaint.

Surety: A person who agrees to be liable for the debt or contractual obligations of another.

Statutory fee: Administrative cost of closing a loan.

Tenancy in common: The common and undivided ownership of property.

Tenancy by the entirety: The joint ownership of property by a husband and wife.

Term: Length of time designated for total repayment of loan.

Testator: A person who makes a will.

Third-party transaction: Involves a buyer, seller, and a lender.

Title search: A check of public records to determine current ownership of a parcel of real estate.

Trustee: A person responsible for the property or affairs of another person, company, or institution.

Unsecured note: A loan granted on the basis of a borrower's creditworthiness and signature; it is not secured by collateral.

Usury: The charge of illegal interest.

Wage assignment: An agreement permitting a lender to collect a certain portion of a borrower's salary from his employer if payment is not made as specified in the credit contract.

Warranty: The representation that an article has certain properties, the breach of which subjects one to financial liability.